"I know what it's like to live exhausted. ⅃ to have Jesus set me free from stress and striving. If that's what you long for too, Glynnis is here to help. Her words are encouraging, practical, and a lifeline for the worn-out and weary."

—**Holley Gerth**, *Wall Street Journal* bestselling author
of *You're Already Amazing*

"There is a good kind of busy that leads to a peaceful, productive, fulfilling life. But there's also a bad kind of busy that throws you into overdrive and unravels your purpose. *Doing Busy Better* will help you tell the difference between the two, liberating your schedule and your soul."

—**Arlene Pellicane**, speaker and author
of *31 Days to Becoming a Happy Mom*

"I love Glynnis's books because I relate to her. I'm wired like her. We task-masters run the risk of burnout. We're also tempted, as Glynnis says, to draw a straight line between our work and our worth. We're often misunderstood by those who cannot relate to our 'manage-much' mindset. But we're not the only ones who battle busyness in unhealthy ways. It's a cultural thing. We live in a fast-paced, rat-race society that values yes over no, busy over bored, and results over fruit. Is there a better way to do busy? Yes! Read this book. You'll be encouraged, validated, and inspired to redeem the time in a way that fits who God made you to be and what He's called you to do."

—**Susie Larson**, talk radio host, national speaker,
and author of *Your Powerful Prayers*

"What do I love most about this book? That a book about busy is *not* written by a woman who took a year off to slow down and 'really' experience what unhurried feels like. This book was written in the trenches, in the midst of real life, by a woman who is wired for busy—but who has learned to do busy as God intended.

Glynnis, thank you for celebrating what God-centered busyness looks like, showing us how to focus on the business that God has intended, and giving us permission to enjoy a productive ministry, home, and career. I will now officially stop apologizing for being busy, as long as my busy is on God's behalf and on His schedule. Highly recommended."

—**Kathi Lipp**, author of the *Publishers Weekly* bestseller *The Husband Project*, *Clutter Free*, and *Overwhelmed*

"My inner 'Martha' struggle is strong. I'm grateful for Glynnis being the voice in my ear that is not scolding my struggle but serving me a solution that is real and refreshing. If you are busy (and let's face it, we all are) this book will be a lifeline of encouragement for your weary soul."

—**Stacey Thacker**, author of *Fresh Out of Amazing*

"Our culture simultaneously screams two messages: 'Get moving! Crank it out. Be busy and productive,' and also 'Slow down and savor. Don't be in such a hurry!' Are these directives mutually exclusive? If so, which one do we obey? Or maybe we were actually created to do both—just not at the same time. In *Doing Busy Better*, Glynnis Whitwer shows us how intentionally adopting a life rhythm of working smart and then resting deeply isn't just healthy for our physical bodies but can also nurture our often-neglected souls. With biblical insight and practical suggestions, this inspiring and helpful book will enable you to stop rushing and start resting while still getting your tasks completed on time."

—**Karen Ehman**, Proverbs 31 Ministries speaker, *New York Times* bestselling author of *Keep It Shut* and *Love, Repeat*, wife, and mother of three

Doing Busy Better

Also by Glynnis Whitwer

Taming the To-Do List

Doing Busy Better

ENJOYING GOD'S GIFTS OF WORK AND REST

Glynnis Whitwer

Revell

a division of Baker Publishing Group
Grand Rapids, Michigan

Published by Revell
a division of Baker Publishing Group
P.O. Box 6287, Grand Rapids, MI 49516-6287
www.revellbooks.com

Printed in the United States of America

Library of Congress Cataloging-in-Publication Data is on file at the Library of Congress, Washington, DC.

978-0-8007-2715-4

Unless otherwise indicated, Scripture quotations are from the Holy Bible, New International Version®. NIV®. Copyright © 1973, 1978, 1984, 2011 by Biblica, Inc.™ Used by permission of Zondervan. All rights reserved worldwide. www.zondervan.com

Scripture quotations labeled ESV are from The Holy Bible, English Standard Version® (ESV®), copyright © 2001 by Crossway, a publishing ministry of Good News Publishers. Used by permission. All rights reserved. ESV Text Edition: 2011

Scripture quotations labeled NCV are from the New Century Version®. Copyright © 2005 by Thomas Nelson, Inc. Used by permission. All rights reserved.

Published in association with the literary agency of Fedd & Company, Inc., P.O. Box 341973, Austin, TX 78734

17 18 19 20 21 22 23   7 6 5 4 3 2 1

This book is dedicated to my sister,
Helen Ann Swett Ferrel,
who modeled loving people more than
projects every day of her life on earth.

Contents

One

The Undercurrent of Unease

It was always there, humming below the surface. Or maybe a low-decibel background noise like conversation at a coffeehouse, the drone of traffic, or the whirring of a ceiling fan. You know, the kind of sound so constant you become immune to it. But when it stops, the quiet seems like a stranger.

That's what I felt for years, but it wasn't a sound. It was a feeling. Maybe more like an undercurrent of unease, a sense that I should be doing something . . . all . . . the . . . time.

No matter what I was doing at the time, how important it was, or how much it needed my utmost focus, my mind hopscotched to something else on my to-do list. Or even more distracting, something that I needed to put on that list. Fear that I would forget kept it looping in my mind.

With that kind of mental drill sergeant at work, who can slow down, pause, or fully focus on the beauty of the moment?

When I did dare to stop, the sergeant sent his associate, Corporal Guilt Thrower, to make sure I didn't rest for long.

For years I simply had too much to do. Much more than one person could handle at once. When you've packed your schedule so tight there's no margin, breathing room, or thinking room—and definitely no room for missteps—it requires constant vigilance to keep that kind of life on the tracks.

And fun? Well, that was pretty hard to fit in. When you are that busy, fun is a hard-to-justify extravagance.

As if thinking about and managing what I needed to do wasn't enough, I thought about and managed what others needed to do. God gave me a wonderful husband and five children. They are all smart and capable, and yet five out of six of them have a severe forgetfulness gene.

I know all the parenting and boundary books (written by people obviously much smarter than me) tell you to allow logical consequences to happen and people will eventually learn coping techniques to manage themselves. But you have to read those books to know that information. And I was too busy to read those books.

So until I read those books my life consisted of daily reminders of assignments and tasks, nonstop hunting for things lost, and frantically helping someone finish something at the last minute.

Whew! Not only did I overload myself, but then I took on the responsibility for everyone in my family. I'm not sure why I stopped there—I mean, why not just take on the responsibility of the world while I'm at it?

Some folks go through *seasons* of overcommitment, usually because of something wonderfully good or terribly hard. Weddings, babies, moves, or illness can interrupt a well-ordered life and introduce chaos for a while.

There are honest reasons why some seasons of life are too busy. Sometimes circumstances collide and there's nothing to do but race to get things done.

From the glad to the sad, life's events can consume us at times.

From the glad to the sad, life's events can consume us at times. But when those times are past, if at our very core we are living in a healthy rhythm of life, we find ourselves returning to that rhythm.

That's not what happened to me.

Let's Just Call It an Addiction

I would call my situation *chronic* overcommitment—moving from one rushed deadline to the next, with no downtime in between.

Some might even have called me addicted to busyness. I've never had an addiction before, so I'm not sure what it might feel like. But if it feels like a constant inner drive to seek out a source of comfort or pleasure, then maybe addiction is the right label.

For most of my life I lived with no margin. There was always something more I wanted to experience, learn, or achieve, or I wanted my children to experience, learn, or achieve. And so when an opportunity arose, my hand would shoot in the air with confident bravado and I'd say yes to something new.

13

Overconfident in my ability to make it work, and with some creative maneuvering in my schedule, I felt certain I could pull this new thing off.

Yes, I'll codirect vacation Bible school the week after my baby is due.

Yes, I'll take on that new responsibility at work.

Yes, I'll lead that committee.

Yes, I can have three sons on three different football teams in the same season. And a daughter on the cheerleading team.

Yes, I'll host that party.

At the time of my enthusiastic response, it all seemed so doable. *Really, how much time will it take? Just a few more hours a week. We'll just be more efficient with our mornings. Create a new after-school routine.*

Adrenaline at the excitement of something new fueled me for a while, but reality quickly set in. And once again "hurry up" echoed through the halls as everyone was stressed and pressed into an overbusy lifestyle.

And with that stressed reality came weariness. The kind of soul-deep weariness that hits when the adrenaline is gone. The kind of tired that makes a productive woman dissolve into tears because there are simply too many choices of plants at the garden center. Or tie-dye kits in the craft store.

I don't know how many other women understand this cycle: optimism, saying yes, living at warp speed, feeling overwhelmed, and swearing *this* will never happen again—until it does. Maybe it's only a handful of us. I know it's not everyone. Some women figure out how to pace themselves.

They know when to guard their "yes" and when enough is enough. They are able to fully enjoy the moment, not worrying about what comes next or who is doing what. They know when to set aside the project and have fun. Are they just wired that way? Are they better at making choices? Have they learned the hard way that life is short?

I don't know the answers for sure to those questions. That's what I'm on a journey to discover. Because the hard truth is, none of that pacing or guarding or saying "no" to a new responsibility comes naturally or easy for me.

I like to work. I'm driven to achieve. I like responsibility and being in charge and bringing order to messes. I like being needed and someone asking for my help.

Plus, I'm afraid what might happen—or not happen—if I stop. So I dare not stop.

Not only am I driven to cross things off my to-do list and tackle the next project, I'm also motivated by the fear of what I might miss. What opportunities or experiences will pass me by if I don't jump on them now? There's always the fear that "this" might not happen again.

"This" changes all the time. It can be friendships, volunteer positions, or assignments at work. For example, if my week is jam-packed but a friend I've been wanting to connect with asks me to have lunch, I'm afraid to say no. It's not that I'm worried about hurting her feelings, but what if she doesn't ask again and I miss this chance?

Or if I'm overloaded at work but an opportunity arises that I've been wanting. I'm concerned I won't get another chance if I say no. So I say yes and work overtime to get it done.

The idea that opportunities are scarce pushes me to take on more than I can handle.

And when you combine all those characteristics *without* an understanding of God's plan for rest, you get a perfect storm for being a walking disaster.

And that, my friends, is what this book is about. In spite of all this hardwiring that pushes me to do more, I'm convinced God never meant for me to live nonstop. At the very start of creation God built work and rest into the architecture of our lives in perfect symmetry.

The idea that opportunities are scarce pushes me to take on more than I can handle.

We were created and commanded to work, and we were created and commanded to rest. The problem comes when we don't enjoy both of these two components in our lives.

Both work and rest are sacred, so why do so many of us feel guilty when we are resting? And then, because we know we should take time for ourselves and others, we feel guilty when we are working!

My journey to find this healthy, guilt-free approach to work and rest has been a long one. I haven't figured it all out. I seem to learn one lesson, implement it into my life, then learn another lesson and apply it. Then I get myself overbusy and have to regroup. Two steps forward, one step back.

I've spent years trying to understand why I tend toward overcommitment and why it's so hard for me to rest. And I've wondered if being busy is really bad. Or maybe we need to be busy about the right things and know when to stop being busy.

Thankfully, I am learning. I'm not the crazy woman I was years ago; my family can tell you that.

The reality is, my life is always going to be full. I'm probably always going to be busy; I'm just wired that way. But I don't have to be overbusy.

The promise of an unhurried, productive life calls my name. I want to live with margin and room to breathe while still getting things done. I want to honor the Sabbath, fully trusting that God will help me complete my work in six days. I want to live without the weight of countless deadlines, with plenty of time to hang out with Jesus, family, and friends.

The promise of an unhurried, productive life calls my name.

I have a feeling you do too. There's got to be a way to do busy better than we're doing it now.

Jesus knew we needed to learn to balance work and rest, because apparently even His first-century followers were exhausted. In Matthew 11:28–30, Jesus said, "Come to me, all you who are weary and burdened, and I will give you rest. Take my yoke upon you and learn from me, for I am gentle and humble in heart, and you will find rest for your souls. For my yoke is easy and my burden is light."

I love that Jesus identified our common condition of weariness without specifying how we got that way. This way, the promise of rest applies to all of us.

Isn't it ironic that to find Jesus's offer of true rest, we need to apply an instrument of work—a yoke?

Jesus said His yoke was easy and His burden was light. Those words should be added to some list of great oxymorons somewhere. Kind of like jumbo shrimp or deafening silence.

A yoke was a bar of wood linking two oxen. Usually the farmer linked a bigger, stronger ox with a younger, weaker one. The strength of the stronger animal allowed the weaker one to accomplish more than it would alone and without bearing the full weight of the work. The stronger ox assumed more of the responsibility so the weaker one wouldn't be crushed.

When we take on Jesus's yoke, He carries the bulk of the weight for us in all areas of our lives. We aren't solely responsible anymore. He guides us and leads us so we aren't crushed. And in doing so we learn from Him a way of life characterized by peace and joy. We find it's possible to work and yet have deep spiritual and physical rest. We find His expectations aren't anything like ours. They don't add extra burdens that are impossible to fulfill.

Nowhere in Scripture do we find the kind of franticness that characterizes some of our lives. We do find lots of messed-up folks, but that's usually when they've decided to try life their way.

When we do life God's way, there is a pleasant sense of order, with enough time to do everything we need to do and everything we are called to do. Jesus certainly modeled that. Just look at all He accomplished in the three years of His recorded ministry, and yet we never read about Him being frazzled.

There are no recorded times of Him yelling at His disciples, "Stop goofing off and get a move on! We've got lots to do."

Instead, in the midst of the needs and demands, especially when people clamored for help, we hear Him say, "Come with me by yourselves to a quiet place and get some rest" (Mark 6:31).

Oh, how I long for that way of life. And I have a feeling you do too.

I'm convinced it's possible. There must be a way to do busy better. There's absolutely too much to do in God's kingdom for us to *not* be busy about our Father's business . . . but there's too much to do to not rest and recharge in the presence of Jesus.

Maybe we need to live more in the center of this oxymoron, this light burden and easy yoke.

This is the way of Jesus. And today He invites all of us who are feeling worried and burdened, from whatever has made us feel overwhelmed, exhausted, and guilty, to come with Him. That's the best place to start. Because although I'm going to do my best to share practices and principles for doing busy better in your life, nothing compares to the soul rest Jesus offers.

There's absolutely too much to do in God's kingdom for us to not be busy about our Father's business . . . but there's too much to do to not rest and recharge in the presence of Jesus.

Now that we've taken care of first things first, let's get started with the idea of being busy. It's a condition most of us experience and yet feel helpless to manage. What drives us to live like this?

Two

What Drives Us to an Overbusy Life?

Although I tend to point at external conditions as the cause for my crazy life, the truth is the worst pressure comes from inside. I'm my own worst enemy. My expectations about myself, my abilities, my stamina, tend toward unrealistic.

Maybe you feel ready to quit, to give up on your job, your ministry, your marriage, because that feels like the only way out. Maybe you feel that kind of apathy coming on, and you are hoping—praying—to fend it off.

I don't know what got you to this point, but I have an idea because I've been there many times before and for many reasons. Although I don't know your exact circumstances, I do think I know what you want. There's a longing in every overbusy woman's heart to press pause, breathe deeply, and soak in the sacred moments of life.

Because He is the Prince of Peace, God has planted within our souls a longing for peace. A life of ordered simplicity. Increased focus. But the everyday demands leave us feeling splintered. Distracted. Restless.

It's too easy for a hurried pace to set the pattern for our days, leaving a trail of rushed relationships and shallow thoughts.

> *It's too easy for a hurried pace to set the pattern for our days, leaving a trail of rushed relationships and shallow thoughts.*

And yet, just when I think I'm doomed to feeling out of control and overloaded with guilt, I get a taste of God's plan for me. I sense its possibilities. For a moment I press pause and discover I'm not a victim of a crazy schedule. I have choices. Yes, certain things are out of my control. But not everything.

And in those moments, when I discover a slower rhythm, when my mind clears of the confusion, when I sense God's nearness, my heart sighs in relief.

This—this life of having enough time to do what God wants us to do—is possible. I know because I've experienced it.

I wish I could say I've got this overbusy thing under control. Some days are better than others. But what I'm learning is no one is too driven, too overwhelmed, or too unfocused to find a greater sense of peace and control in their lives. We serve the God of all-things-are-possible! His ways are not frantic or overloaded, and He will guide us toward a life that reflects His peace. If we let Him, I believe God will start to remove the chains that have kept us bound to an overwhelmed life.

Let me warn you, there will be work to do, but not the time-consuming kind. In order to regain control of our schedules, we'll need to make some changes. But before we make any external decisions, let's start by looking internally, because the first and most important change needs to start with us. Before we can ever make lasting changes, we'll need to figure out what got us to this place of overload. Spoiler alert: it's not a demanding boss or precious children.

Our Drives and Desires

We all have an internal drive. It's that motivation that pushes us to do what we do and prompts how we spend time and money.

Our drives are always connected with desires. We desire connection so we spend time with friends. We desire to be beautiful so we spend money on cosmetics and clothes. We desire comfort and security so we redecorate the living room or watch Hallmark movies. We desire excitement so we travel.

Sometimes our internal drive moves us toward good things. We want a relationship with God so we spend time in prayer. We want to care for those in need so we volunteer. We want to be healthy so we exercise.

Then there are internal drives that move us toward self-defeating or harmful choices. And this is where things get complicated. As self-protecting as we all are, why would we do things that are self-defeating? Why would any of us make harmful decisions?

Wouldn't you like to know the answer to that? If I knew that answer, I'd be at my goal weight now. I'd keep my mouth shut when I start feeling defensive at work. And I'd take advantage of teachable moments with my children rather than rush through them.

Just imagine if we all made decisions in our best interest . . . there'd be no credit card debt, no broken marriages, and no health problems due to inactivity. We'd be much happier and healthier people.

But we don't.

Identifying the Benefit

We might point to external factors as the reason why we make our choices. But that's seldom the whole truth.

For example, for years I believed I could lay the blame for being late on my children. And there is some truth to that. Children are full of surprises, and their thinking is age-appropriate. That's why they lose things we can't imagine losing. Like the shoes they took off when they walked in the house five minutes earlier. Or the homework they were working on right before dinner.

There were many school mornings we ran late because— surprise!—someone announced at 7:00 a.m. they were Superstar of the Week and had to bring a poster with photos of themselves and family members and cupcakes for the class. Today! Or they would lose their chance for the rest of the year.

But when I'm gut honest with myself, the real reason I ran late is I was always trying to squeeze one more thing into our packed schedule and trying to check one more thing off my to-do list. Or, rather than preparing the night before, I mentally checked out due to my exhausting day.

Extrapolate that thinking to my life on a larger scale, and it's easy to see why I've lived a majority of my life, not just my mornings, on overload. No matter how much I'm doing or what deadlines I face, I think I can squeeze one more thing on my to-do list.

You see, external forces can confirm our internal drives, but seldom are they to blame for our self-defeating choices. The blame, if you want to call it that, lies on our unhealthy inner drives.

Years ago I remember watching Dr. Phil talk to a sobbing woman. She was tired of being angry all the time. He told her that to deal with her anger once and for all, she had to identify the benefit from being angry.

"There's no benefit!" she wailed. "I don't want to get angry with my kids and my husband and my friends! They don't want to be with me. There's no benefit in that!"

It was eye-opening when Dr. Phil went on to explain she gets a benefit when she experiences the power to control the conversation or the circumstance. Even though it's unhealthy, it's still a benefit.

The same is true for us. We get a benefit when we live overloaded lives, although it certainly isn't healthy. We might feel important or valued. We might feel power and influence.

For some of us brought up in the church, we might be driven to do good works because we believe we earn God's love or approval when we do the right things. In that case, the benefit is assurance we are in God's good graces. This is righteousness by works, and that drives many followers of Jesus to do more.

I've spent years trying to understand what drives me to overwork, and upon review, it seems there have been different drives at different seasons of my life. But when I retrace my steps, the foundation of all my motivation to do more starts with my internal wiring to be responsible.

I've taken pride in being the responsible one from an early age. I was the child my parents didn't have to worry about, the student the teacher could depend on, the friend who would do what she said, and the employee who was always on time.

However, my responsibility didn't affect my being overbusy until I went to college.

It was in college when I realized my work was never done. There was always more to read, read again, research, or review. I never felt prepared enough for the next class, assignment, or test, so I'd fill in every spare moment with study.

There was no college fund set aside, so I put myself through college working one and sometimes two jobs. I felt like I needed to work more hours for financial security.

I knew I needed to have something to put on a résumé, so I joined a few clubs, got an internship, and wrote for the school paper. I even became president of the Public Relations Student Society of America, attending professional meetings when I could.

To say those years were jam-packed is an understatement. I know lots of people had this experience, so my college years weren't unique. But my inability to slow down was different.

Something took hold of me in college that I hadn't experienced before and became the foundation for a way of life. Like two little monkeys clambering up my back, responsibility and guilt grabbed hands and prodded me to do more. I didn't dare stop working.

I wasn't always like this. I wasn't the one in grade school or high school to belong to every club. No overachiever gene lurks in my DNA. I wasn't driven to be the class president or valedictorian. School wasn't a breeze for me; I worked hard for my grades.

I was still under my parents' care back then. I trusted them to provide for me, so I didn't feel quite so driven. It really was quite a delightful experience.

But when I got to college, I felt the full weight of the responsibility for my life—both then and in the future. No one was going to get my degree, get me a job, and find a place for me to live but me.

It was hard to relax when there was no end to the work I could do. And so I didn't. Relax, that is. Between working part-time jobs and managing a full-time load of classes, the guilt hounded me any time I stopped working.

Even when I wasn't working, I wasn't resting, because my mind was always abuzz, thinking of what I needed to do next. Or what I should have done better. Beating myself up over yesterday's mistakes and strategizing how to do better tomorrow became a way of life.

There was some fun in college, but only because I met my husband, Tod, there. And while his work drive is similar to mine, he has this manly ability to compartmentalize his life. School went in this basket, work in that basket, and a burgeoning relationship with me in another basket. And when he decided to stop studying or working, he actually could have fun.

It took some compelling on his part, but eventually I gave in and had some fun too. Sort of. Because even then I was always aware of the time, always aware of the potential traffic after we left the venue, and I found myself thinking about what time I had to get up the next day and when I should stop having fun.

Busy was my byline. Guilt was my narrative.

But I also lived with hope. This beautiful, unrealistic hope that once I got past the next deadline, I'd be able to relax for a bit. This hope pushed me through many long nights and constant rushing from one thing to the next, until I collapsed in exhaustion, legs and back aching from my job as a waitress, eyes blurry and neck stiff from bending over a desk.

An interesting reality exists when you put your hope of rest in completing a project: there's always another project waiting for you to finish whatever you're working on now.

An interesting reality exists when you put your hope of rest in completing a project: there's always another project waiting for you to finish whatever you're working on now.

The queue of projects and tasks is never-ending, one after the other, waiting for you. Kind of like a line of elephants, trunks holding tails. Sometimes they wait silently. Other times your next project stamps its feet in irritation. But they are always waiting, threatening to crush you should you fall behind.

As if a job and a full class load weren't enough, Tod proposed, and somehow we decided we could squeeze a wedding and honeymoon in before my senior year of classes started. So rather than enjoying some downtime in the summer, and with help from parents and friends, we pulled off a simple ceremony and reception just ten days before classes started.

My bridesmaids and I made all the corsages and boutonnieres. I picked up the grocery-store wedding cake. Sweet church ladies set out bowls of pink and green mints and nuts, and poured punch that we made fancy by mixing in sherbet.

After a quick honeymoon, we moved in to our apartment on a weekend, we started back at school, I added a second part-time job, and we took off again full throttle.

Our Internal Motor Is Always Running

You probably have your own story of when your life got crazy. And right now maybe you're thinking of what drives you. Some of you are identifying for the first time that we share a similar internal driving force of responsibility.

Miss Responsibility. So exciting, right? There are no high school awards given for *that* personality trait.

I'm definitely not the one to invite to a party, unless you want someone to pick up other people's cups before they leave a mark on the furniture. Or worry about how people are getting home if they've had anything to drink. In fact, you might invite me if you want someone to organize the potluck to make sure no one brings the same dish.

Responsibility is a good characteristic to have, especially when it's in other people. They are the ones who do what they say, and you can count on them when you have a problem.

But when you are the responsible one, it's hard to draw clear boundary lines between what is your responsibility and what is not. So everything feels like your responsibility.

Responsibility fuels my inner motor, but it might not fuel yours. You might find yourself driven to exhaustion by the need to prove yourself, earn the approval of others, have value, or build a career. Some people are driven by pleasing others, some by rewards, some by recognition.

Fear might fuel you to overwork. You might be afraid of missed opportunities, financial troubles, or someone else getting what you want. There are so many reasons we fill our schedules to overflowing and push ourselves (and others) to the max.

Your internal motor is always humming just beneath the surface, consuming your thoughts. It's what pushes you to write lists, make plans, and strategize, all to manage the amount of work you have to do. It's like you're a race car without "neutral" and definitely no "park."

As I mentioned in chapter 1, sometimes life happens in a rush, with circumstances overlapping. We all have these times that make us feel crazy. However, when this life becomes the norm, we can be sure we're dealing with something else.

That's when it becomes chronic busyness.

And if you "slack off" (which is what we overbusy types call watching TV on a Saturday afternoon when there's housework or yard work to be done) you are being lazy. And then the second little monkey, guilt, sneaks in.

Will I Ever Not Feel Guilty?

Ah, guilt. My lifelong companion. Guilt motivates me to work, and then I feel guilty for working *too hard*. Guilt motivates me to take a break, and then I feel guilty for *not* working.

Interestingly, responsibility and guilt are connected, because guilt is defined as the *responsibility* of an individual or group for an offense or wrongdoing—as in, the *guilty* party. So guilt can occur when there is a wrong thought, word, or action.

But guilt also carries with it an internal sense of being wrong, not just doing wrong. And for someone who tries so very hard to *do* right and *be* right, being constantly wrong is crushing.

I feel guilty about not spending more time on a project at work and not spending enough time with my children. I feel guilty for overcommitting to some things and for not committing enough to other things.

Then there's the guilt of not writing my sponsored Compassion International child enough, not volunteering to support veterans, not walking in the Susan G. Komen three-day walk, not helping my sister with a problem, not doing more to promote my own books, and so on! And then there are so many books and magazine articles out there about how bad it is to be busy, I feel even worse.

But this guilt isn't even true guilt. Guilt is when someone actually does something wrong. I feel guilty over things that aren't wrong. I only think I should have done them. Like when I wished I'd reviewed a project at work more carefully or spent more time with my mother.

Guilt is never content to settle on one person. A person who feels guilty desperately tries to lessen the feeling

Guilt is never content to settle on one person.

by bringing others into that condition as well, using guilt to manipulate people or circumstances. And so the cycle continues.

It's an exhausting way to live.

If you are reading this and have lived your life on fast-forward for too long, you completely understand this relentless drive and the guilt. And you know the weariness that accompanies it all.

And you wish you knew when enough was enough.

Friend, you've come to the right place. First, you've come to a place where there will be no more guilt or shame heaped on you for what you've done or haven't done. Maybe we haven't done everything right; we've made mistakes, but we don't stand accused.

For those things we have truly done wrong, Jesus has taken on our guilt. He has paid our price before God through His death on the cross. When we have truly repented of our sins, God is faithful to forgive us. So our guilt is GONE!

Any guilt we feel after that does not belong to us. We have an enemy of our souls who would like to chain us to guilt, because he knows that guilt will always cause us to do one of two things: work hard to earn forgiveness, or give up in defeat.

We are assuming guilt for things we haven't done wrong. This false guilt is crippling because there's nothing for God to forgive, so we never have the sense of forgiveness. We condemn ourselves and live with a quiet sense of shame and failure.

But look what the Scriptures say about this kind of condemnation. Romans 8:1 says, "There is therefore now no condemnation for those who are in Christ Jesus" (ESV). John 3:17 says, "For God did not send his Son into the world to condemn the world, but in order that the world might be saved through him" (ESV).

And this might be my favorite verse on condemnation: "This is how we know that we belong to the truth and how we set our hearts at rest in his presence: If our hearts condemn us, we know that God is greater than our hearts, and he knows everything" (1 John 3:19–20).

If you've been living with guilt for too long, this promise of a heart at rest is sweet. And as we'll discover together, true rest starts in our hearts and souls. We'll never find rest if we associate it with checking something off our to-do list. And that is the second thing you'll find here: an opportunity to build guilt-free rest into your life. This won't be easy if you've been on overload for a long time. We actually can feel powerless to make a change. But the idea of rest is so biblical, we can take it as both a gift and a promise from God for us.

There's one more idea I want to share right at the start: *Busy isn't bad.* I hope that's a relief to those of you wired to work. The Bible is clear we were created to do good work in this life. Productivity is praised, and we are cautioned against laziness. But some of us need to learn that taking time to rest is not the same as being lazy. And while being busy isn't bad, being overbusy is often counterproductive.

I'm convinced that when we learn the idea of biblical rest, it will break our addiction to a nonstop lifestyle. And in doing so, we will come to understand the idea of the abundant life Jesus promised in John 10:10: "The thief comes only to steal and kill and destroy. I came that they may have life and have it abundantly" (ESV).

Being driven to overwork isn't a twenty-first-century problem. To Jesus's listeners, life was a series of rules and regulations. Jesus knew they felt bound by expectations too. They had to live right to be right. When you think about it, that's not far off from life today. Our lives are filled with lists and deadlines. We've got to get it all done to feel right.

But Jesus wasn't offering a life of getting more done. That's not the kind of abundance He meant. In John 10:11, Jesus describes Himself as a "good shepherd." All those listening would have known immediately what a good shepherd does, and we have Psalm 23 to help us understand it too.

I'd like to end this chapter with Psalm 23. And if you are feeling worn out today, allow the Good Shepherd to care tenderly for you:

> The LORD is my shepherd, I lack nothing.
> He makes me lie down in green pastures,
> he leads me beside quiet waters,
> he refreshes my soul.
> He guides me along the right paths
> for his name's sake.
>
> Even though I walk
> through the darkest valley,
> I will fear no evil,
> for you are with me;
> your rod and your staff,
> they comfort me.
>
> You prepare a table before me
> in the presence of my enemies.
> You anoint my head with oil;
> my cup overflows.
> Surely your goodness and love will follow me
> all the days of my life,
> and I will dwell in the house of the LORD
> forever.

Three

Being versus Doing

For many years, I had the ability to move from success to disappointment in a heartbeat. Just when I thought I had it all together, something happened. I'd forget an appointment. Snap at one of my children. Or procrastinate on a project until I was stressed out and mad.

Because of my internal drive to be responsible, I took pride in what I accomplished and had developed a very independent streak. I bought into the lie that "success" in anything depended on me.

That's a dangerous way to live, because although I loved and served God, I didn't really think I needed Him very much. Ahem . . . may I clearly state for the record that I *did* need God, and I needed Him more desperately than I even knew.

After years of doing things my way, I'd built my identity on the shaky foundation of my circumstances and abilities.

If the press release I wrote for a grand opening got picked up by the newspaper, I felt great. If it didn't, I felt like a failure.

If the women's ministry event I helped plan had a good attendance, my confidence was high. If registration was lower than expected, I was certain it was because of something I didn't do.

As soon as the delicate balance of my identity was tipped with a mistake, misstep, or mishap, I kicked it into overdrive to try and compensate. But all that frenetic activity never made a lasting difference.

My roller-coaster identity took me on a wild ride for years, but not the fun theme-park kind. Basically I had connected my *being* and my *doing*. These two things are opposite, but somehow I had connected them: I was what I did. And how I felt about myself was connected with how well I performed.

You can imagine when your identity is wrapped up in what you do, you will always seek to do more. Every project, assignment, or goal has an ending, so you are always on the hunt for the next thing to accomplish.

When you are in the throes of this race to maintain your identity, it's almost impossible to label it as such. It just seems like good works, and what's wrong with *that*?

Sometimes it takes having it all pulled out from underneath you for you to see clearly. And that's what happened to me.

Shortly after we married, Tod and I put a five-year plan in place. In that time we would both graduate, develop our careers, buy a house, and then we would start our family. The plan started off well.

Once we finished school, we both found full-time jobs and dove headfirst into our church involvement. And boy, oh boy, were we involved. If my college years were busy, they were only a warm-up for the years to come.

We immediately got invited to lead the senior high youth group and joined a young couples' Bible study. We also helped start a Wednesday evening children's program and served on the evangelism committee. Then I joined the choir, sang in the praise band, and helped lead women's ministry.

It's actually embarrassing to type all that out, because it is such a picture of my longing for significance. And if you can believe it, it was about to get worse.

Even with all that busyness, we didn't forget our plan. So at the end of five years, we started trying to have a family. This is where our plans began to derail, as we learned getting pregnant wasn't as easy as flipping an "on" switch.

One year passed, and doctors stamped "infertility" on my charts. Year two passed with lots of infertility tests and thoughts of adoption filling our days. Year three was almost past when, with the help of a doctor, our first son became more than a dream.

Nine months later, Joshua Owen Whitwer changed the world as I knew it . . . forever. And my search for significance in what I did shifted into overdrive.

I adored my little son and loved him more than I thought possible. But I never considered changing my other life plans for him. After a short maternity break, I returned to work.

Apparently the infertility issues were in the past, because twenty-six months later Dylan was born, and twenty-one months after that, Robbie joined the family.

Before Joshua was born, I had decided to keep up my prechild pace of activity and involvement once he arrived. I didn't see why I should slow down or cut back on anything. I wanted to be the mother who could do it all.

Only no one told my children they needed to cooperate with the plan. And when Robbie refused to take a bottle or sleep through the night for ten months, I started to realize I might not be able to control my life like I thought.

J didn't see why J should slow down or cut back on anything. J wanted to be the mother who could do it all.

I couldn't go anywhere without him for more than a few hours. And even after he was able to drink from a bottle, my little Robbie decided he preferred me over anyone.

The next three years were the hardest of my life. Frustration reigned in my heart and mind as I tried to regain my "old life." But I couldn't do anything like before.

It was like trying to walk upstream . . . in mud . . . to my knees . . . carrying three children in my arms. Let's just say it wasn't graceful. But I'll tell you more about that in a later chapter. For now, I want you to get a picture of the woman I was: an administratively inclined leader with control issues who was involved with everything.

Although every day was a struggle, I envisioned life returning to "normal" when Robbie started school. Still, it was a good life. The boys were healthy, Tod had a good career, and my job allowed me to work part-time. I was active in church, sang in the choir, and led children's and parts of women's ministries. My parents and two of my sisters lived close by, and we had a snug little house with a fenced pool in the backyard.

When God Decides to Get Your Attention

One day, Tod came home with news that his company was closing their Phoenix office. He was the manager and had only been with them ten months. They offered him a job in Denver, but we weren't interested in moving. At least that's what I thought.

Tod had a few months to close up the office and find a new position. We weren't really worried, because being a consultant, Tod had many professional connections in Phoenix. However, I was completely unprepared for what happened next.

Tod received a call from a friend who had moved to North Carolina. This friend had a job he wanted Tod to consider. I had no interest or plans to move, but Tod wanted to at least check it out. So he flew back there, all the while saying, "I'm not interested, I just want to see what he has to say."

Can you guess what happened next? A job offer, stormy conversations, lots of tears, then we packed up, rented out our house, and moved to Charlotte, North Carolina. An important part of this story is that my husband wanted to move back to Phoenix in two or three years.

That makes it sound much neater than it really was. The long version is I was a bitter, angry, and resentful woman. The injustice of the situation consumed me. I was convinced moving was not in God's will for me, and I told my husband so. With one hand on my hip and another pointed at him, I told him, "Just because your name rhymes with God doesn't mean you know His will!"

Yep, it wasn't pretty.

Even though my husband only wanted to move for a few years, it made no difference. I continually asked myself, *How could he be so selfish? How could he ask me to move across the country and leave everything I love—my work, my ministry, my family?*

Yet a feather-like thought tickled inside. I knew Tod had never demanded his way in the past, and in fact, he wasn't demanding now. If I said no, then we wouldn't move. But I also knew that if I said no, then I would be squelching a dream he'd had for many years, which was to live in a different city. And next time it could be a less desirable destination.

Then I heard God clearly tell me, "Your husband has never demanded his way; it's his time. Tell him *yes*." I knew that thought didn't come from me, because that was the opposite of what I wanted to do. Deep in my heart, I knew it was God.

You'd think I'd be overjoyed to hear God so clearly. For years I heard other people talk about God speaking directly to them, but I'd never experienced it. I wanted Him to speak to me! *But why did the first thing He say to me have to be about this? Why didn't God tell me to treat myself to a new outfit or a pedicure? Not move across the country!* But that was God's command.

In a moment of teeth-gritting determination and with a fearful heart, I said yes and committed to not complain, and we moved. But in my heart, I was a mess. I'm ashamed to say that I believed my husband had stepped so far out of God's plan that I was destined to suffer for the next two years.

While I was outwardly submissive, inwardly my heart was darkly rebellious. I decided to make the best of it, get through the next few years, and then return to my real life. I believed that when I returned to Arizona, I would go back to work and continue to serve God in my usual capacity.

I tried hard not to complain, but it's amazing how a woman can let her man know she's not happy without ever saying a word. I moped a lot. And in my heart, I was bitter and resentful. My thought life was like a flushing toilet, constantly swirling, filled with unmentionables, and going down.

Could It Get Any Worse?

We moved two thousand miles from the desert of Phoenix to the beautiful green of Charlotte, and you would think just the sheer beauty of it would cheer me up. But nope. Tod had picked out this beautiful Southern house with a deck, a garden, and a playhouse in the backyard, and I stood on that back deck one of our first nights there and literally told him I had no joy.

The boys were three, five, and seven at that time, and the busyness of the move and getting the older two started in school kept my mind occupied temporarily. But I was overwhelmed with sadness, to the point I just wanted to cry all the time. We carried a box of tissues in the car, and the kids learned to just hand me one without saying a word.

I was lonely for sure. But that wasn't all of it. What hit me harder than anything was feeling like a nobody, a nothing, with no value to anyone.

You see, I never had a self-esteem problem until I had no way to prove what I could do. No one knew what my talents were—that I could sing, that I could write, that I could successfully organize a special event. All my accomplishments and achievements meant nothing.

When every accomplishment was stripped away, what was left was an unhappy, self-centered woman who didn't think

God could make anything good out of a miserable situation. Instead of seeing what I had, all I could see was what I didn't have—and mainly that was something to do.

When I wasn't crying, I was trying to make some kind of a home to live in. These were the days before HGTV, so one day, while I was shopping at a Christian bookstore, I found a book called *No Ordinary Home* by author Carol Brazo. It was subtitled *The Uncommon Art of Christ-Centered Homemaking*.

Since I was going to be a full-time homemaker for a few years, I thought that book might help me. And since I didn't have a church or workplace in which to prove myself, maybe I could accomplish something in my home.

God had a surprise in store for me.

What I learned from reading the book was more than how to manage a home. Rather than focusing on the practical side of caring for a home, the author had learned a lesson I needed to learn too. And thankfully, she wrote it down.

I had no idea God was about to shake up my life in the very best way when I learned a life-changing truth about how He sees me and how I should see myself. Brazo says:

> If there were one biblical truth I wish I could give my children and lay hold of in my own deepest parts, it would be this one thing. He created me, He loves me, He will always love me. Nothing I do will change who I am.
>
> Being versus doing. The error was finally outlined in bold. I was always worried about what I was doing.
>
> God's only concern was and is what I am being—a child of His, forgiven, justified by the work of His Son, His heir.
>
> He did everything that needed doing; I need to relax and concentrate on being. The only thing I need to do is come to grips with God's way of seeing me.[1]

Being versus Doing

Being versus doing. Those three simple words pierced my heart. The book dropped in my lap as tears filled my eyes. She was talking about me. I was always worried about what I was doing too.

It was like blinders were removed from my eyes, and I could see it all clearly. For all those years I drove myself and my family crazy trying to do it all; what I really wanted was to feel valued . . . to feel like I was worth something.

Being versus doing—those three words redefined my understanding of what God wanted of me. It's hard to describe the thunderbolt of understanding that hit me. It was as if God took a key, turned the lock, and removed the heavy chains of expectation I'd bound myself with.

God wasn't done with the lesson I needed to learn. Within weeks of learning that truth about myself, and through a series of events only He could orchestrate, God connected me with Proverbs 31 Ministries.

It was probably not a coincidence that God connected me with a Christian women's organization based in Charlotte whose tagline at that time was "Touching Women's Hearts, Building Godly Homes." My heart needed more than touching back then. It needed a good swat.

As I became involved in this ministry, God revealed that my view of my life and purpose was small compared to His. I had separated all the areas of my life and was destroying myself trying to keep everything "balanced." Not only was I suffering, but I shortchanged everyone I loved, including God. It was as if my priorities were upside down.

As the truth of my identity in Christ became a reality in my life, I realized I was not the person God wanted me to be.

The selfishness the move revealed had been there all along. Even though my life looked good on the outside, self-interest motivated much of my life. Did my husband meet my needs? Did my children meet my needs? Did my church meet my needs? Did my job meet my needs? Me, me, me.

God pulled me out of the workplace, out of all my volunteer responsibilities, and away from everything I loved to show me that it wasn't all about me. It was and is all about Jesus and how my heart reflects Him.

The Relentless Pursuit of Identity

When your identity is grounded in your accomplishments, it creates a never-ending cycle of pursuit.

Tasks, projects, jobs, and programs always have an ending. And when one project ends, a woman whose identity is wrapped up in her performance will find another stage on which to perform.

We draw a straight line from our actions to our identity. So when we stumble in any area of our lives, we connect dots that aren't there and call ourselves clumsy, stupid, pathetic.

A woman whose identity is wrapped up in her performance will find another stage on which to perform.

Those aren't lines God draws. Only Satan, the enemy of our souls, draws a line from our work to our worth. Only the enemy wants us to find our identity in what we do, because he knows when the lights dim and the "success" is gone, so is our value.

God, however, has another identity for us, one that's unchanging and independent of our actions. It's as His chosen and beloved children. John 1:12 says, "Yet to all who did receive him, to those who believed in his name, he gave the right to become children of God."

When I first learned this truth about my identity, it took a long time to accept. Each time I caught my belittling self-talk, I had to make a choice about what to believe. I had to choose to take God at His word and believe in His love. This took my faith from academic head knowledge to real-life heart belief.

Only the enemy wants us to find our identity in what we do, because he knows when the lights dim and the "success" is gone, so is our value.

If I have any doubt that God's approval is not conditioned on my perfect behavior, Romans 5:6–8 corrects me with truth:

> You see, at just the right time, when we were still powerless, Christ died for the ungodly. Very rarely will anyone die for a righteous person, though for a good person someone might possibly dare to die. But God demonstrates his own love for us in this: While we were still sinners, Christ died for us.

God's acceptance of us, and hence our identity, is *not* defined by our actions. So we will never be a "failure" when our performance doesn't match our expectations. When we reassign the source of our value and worth to its rightful place, we will be free from the fear of failure or the opinions of others. We will be free from the labels we place on ourselves and free from the shifting sands of our self-worth.

The only thing that matters is what our heavenly Father thinks about us. And that is unchanging. We can rest knowing we are safe and secure in God's unconditional love.

Once we really believe this truth, our identity will be unshakable. And once our identity is secured, we will no longer be women driven to find our worth in what we do. What freedom that will be!

The other benefit to understanding our true identity is that work returns to its healthy place in our lives—to God's original design.

Four

God's Original Design for Work

There's an adage that says, "If the devil can't make you bad, he'll make you busy." Clearly, the person who wrote this and people who repeat it believe being busy is very wrong. But what if God is actually pleased with the *right* kind of busy?

As you can tell by now, I'm a gal who likes to be busy. But just as obvious is the reality I've crossed the line many times from being wisely productive to being overwhelmed. I think that's part of the human condition. We all have the potential to push a good thing to an extreme.

Maybe the problem is we've labeled this extreme condition "busy" when we should call it what it is: frantic, chaotic, or overbusy.

Before we demonize the idea of being busy, let's start by looking at the definition. The first dictionary definition of *busy* seems quite pleasant: "actively and attentively engaged in work or a pastime."[2]

It's too easy to look at our chaotic lives, cluttered homes, and fractured relationships and think the problem must surely be that we are busy. But how can being attentive and engaged cause those problems?

Or maybe we get to the end of a day full of nonstop work and yet have the sense we didn't get anything done. Were we too busy? Or maybe we were busy with the wrong things?

Busy gets a bad rap. And because of that, it leaves many of us feeling like we're doing something wrong when we work hard.

When I refer to work in this book, I want to clarify that I'm referring to whatever responsibilities God has given us. For some this will mean caring for a home, raising children, leading a ministry, participating in athletics, teaching, or being employed. There are so many ways we work.

We live in a culture obsessed with either overwork or underwork. Whatever kind of work we have, some people work too hard and drive themselves into the ground, while others think working hard is a sin and look with judgment on the rest.

As we continue this discussion of how to do busy better, let's take a look at what the Bible says about work. This is a crucial part of the conversation if we want to find the balance between work and rest—and enjoy both.

To fully understand God's intent for work and rest within our lives, we need to go back to the beginning, back to God's first act of work.

The First Reference to Work

The first reference we find to work is attributed to God at creation. After creating the heavens, the earth, and everything in them, Scripture says God rested from His work: "By the seventh day God had finished the work he had been doing; so on the seventh day he rested from all his work" (Gen. 2:2).

At the dawn of creation, in our very first "lesson" about God, we find our heavenly Father working for six days. God definitely modeled active and attentive effort when He created the world.

Just consider the human brain! Or the protective fur on an animal. Or food that grows on trees. God was obviously not distracted while He did this work. Our beautiful world and the people within it were created through God's intentional, attentive work.

But God didn't just work Himself; He also assigned work to His creation.

In the second chapter of Genesis, after God created Adam and Eve, Scripture records, "The LORD God took the man and put him in the Garden of Eden to work it and take care of it" (Gen. 2:15).

Adam was a farmer. What a great first job! But then God also told Adam to name all the animals. Does this make Adam a linguist?

Work was Adam's first responsibility. In fact, it would appear to be the first "call" of God on someone's life.

Why would God make Adam work? Wouldn't it have been easier for Adam to just have fun?

God could have easily made the garden self-sustaining. He could have made nuts without shells and grapes to grow on bushes instead of vines needing a trellis. But God didn't do that. He made the garden so it needed human hands to thrive.

Which means God created Adam with the strength, intelligence, and creativity to care for the garden. God intentionally designed Adam to work and gave him purpose this way.

We also see a beautiful act of trust in this assignment to work. Imagine pouring yourself out to create your finest work, then handing it over to someone else to manage. God's assignment to care for creation was truly a gift to Adam. It showed God's affection and trust.

Work at its finest offers us the same blessings. We are able to use our God-given design, and we experience the pleasure of being given a responsibility. I remember the day my boss called me to ask if I'd be willing to oversee a new department at work. It was something she'd been dreaming about doing for years, and finally she was ready to launch it. The fact that she trusted me with her "baby" and thought me capable made me feel fantastic. I wanted to do a good job not only for myself but to please her.

As we look back to the creation story, we find there was also a limitation God put on Adam regarding the work. There was one tree Adam was supposed to leave alone. Just one! It was the tree of the knowledge of good and evil. "For when you eat from it," God said, "you will certainly die" (Gen. 2:17).

We know now that Adam and Eve couldn't keep their hands off that tree. It's like they marched right to it, dared God to keep them from eating it, and got themselves ensnared with lies.

They were seduced by a serpent who made them question God's commandment and His goodness. They messed up their first work assignment by trusting themselves rather than God and ate from that off-limits tree.

Isn't that so much like us? Tell us what we can't do and it's all we can think about.

I remember the summer my parents rented an apartment in Berkeley, California, so my father could take some classes at the university. I'd never lived in an apartment before, and there was so much that was new, including the red fire alarm that was secured to the wall outside our door.

I knew I wasn't supposed to touch it, but one day while I was waiting alone in the hall, I absolutely had to touch that fire alarm. In fact, it was all I could think about. So I reached my little seven-year-old arm up and pulled the lever!

Immediately I regretted my decision, as the shrieking alarm brought everyone running in panic. And I did the only thing I could think to do—I lied. I told them a little girl who looked just like me pulled that alarm and ran down the hall. I am seriously the worst liar ever.

Thankfully, we didn't get kicked out of the apartment, and I don't even remember getting in trouble. But the embarrassment I felt and the regret of disobedience follow me today.

Adam and Eve's sin had much worse consequences. Their act of disobedience has ricocheted through time, as sin entered our world through their choice. And because of trusting themselves rather than God, among the many consequences they (we) received, God told Adam he would toil painfully in order to eat.

Work was originally meant to be a blessing, but through sin it became tainted.

It's so important for us to look at the original blessing and holiness of work. God never intended for work to be

51

something we tolerate to get to the weekend. It was not supposed to be dreaded. And it was also not supposed to be misused.

God designed work to be a healthy part of our lives. It's how we live out our God-given design and use our gifts and talents. Yet sin leaves us wounded in every area of life, and work is no exception. Sin broke the divine work-rest rhythm God established, so it's not surprising we don't have a healthy view of how these two major components of our lives should complement each other.

Satan still tempts us with false promises about the benefits of work, and here are four lies he plants in our heads:

I have to work this hard to provide for myself.

I have to work this hard to get ahead.

I have to work this hard to give my children opportunities.

Work gives me identity and meaning.

There are so many more lies that prod us to work more than we should, but each of those lies has the same exact root Satan used on Adam and Eve: We are our own providers and we know better than God.

If someone asked me, "Glynnis, do you think you know better than God?" I would say, "Of course not! He's God." And yet, for so many years my life spoke the truth of my real belief. I trusted my own strength, effort, and thoughts rather than God's.

When we feel that our safety, security, and significance depend on us, we will not know when to stop working. We will push ourselves beyond capacity. And we will take on more than we can handle.

The alternative is so simple and yet so hard. It's what God has wanted all along. He wants us to trust Him. Trust Him with our daily needs. Trust Him to open doors of opportunity. Trust Him to define our identity.

If we truly trusted God, we would not look for work to supply our needs. God would be our provider and work would be our calling. And rest would be a gift, not something we resent because it keeps us from working.

When we feel that our safety, security, and significance depend on us, we will not know when to stop working.

The answer to our culture's challenge with finding a balance between work and rest has to be deeper than applying some time-management tips during the week, heading to the lake on Saturday to rest, and using Sunday as a day to catch up on whatever work or chores we missed.

These external answers aren't working. If they were, we wouldn't have so many people identifying themselves as workaholics. We wouldn't have so many of us stressed out, burned out, checked out, and dealing with anxiety issues. I'm not a doctor or psychologist, so I'm not making a sweeping medical statement, but there's something very wrong in how we approach work and rest. Surely our lives would be healthier if we lived more according to God's design for these two key areas.

This is the journey God has had me on for the past few years. He's been trying to teach me that His plan for work was never meant to be a burden. And that His gift of rest is one I shouldn't reject.

Regarding our approach to work, there are four principles we can pull from Scripture to help us return to God's original design. The first we actually find in Proverbs 31 . . . that oft-misunderstood passage of the Old Testament.

Put God First

One of my favorite chapters of the Bible is Proverbs 31. Partly because I've worked for a ministry by that name for almost twenty years, but also because it's a chapter that paints a portrait of a highly productive woman. But the undergirding of all her efforts, and why this chapter makes sense, is found in verse 30: She fears the Lord.

Let's look at the chapter before unpacking verse 30, which has plagued many through misunderstanding.

This chapter is attributed to an unnamed mother who is giving advice to her son, King Lemuel. The first section of Proverbs 31, verses 1–9, is general advice for a king. And I can just hear a mother's voice when I read it: "Don't drink, smoke, or chew, or go with girls who do."

Then the passage transitions into the longest passage in the entire Bible with advice for women, wives specifically. It was originally an acrostic poem with each verse beginning with a consecutive letter of the Hebrew alphabet.

Some momma went to a lot of work to help her son remember the qualities to look for in a fine wife. Most of the principles in Proverbs 31:10–31 can be applied to any woman, married or single.

She works with her hands.

She brings food from afar.

She gets up early in the morning to provide food for her family.

She buys investment property.

She plants a vineyard.

She makes sure her family is well-dressed.

She makes her own bed coverings.

She makes linen garments and sells them.

She helps the needy.

She watches over the affairs of her household.

She's not idle.

Logically, this can't be a checklist for a wife. After all, how many vineyard-growing, garment-making, land-investing women are out there? Rather, tucked within the activities of this productive woman is a list of traits in a woman of noble character. So rest assured, you aren't a failure as a woman if you don't buy land, make quilts, or grow grapes.

What's most important here are the characteristics of a godly woman: one who cares for those she loves and is willing to work hard to provide for her family.

When I look over this list, I see an efficient, hardworking entrepreneur. But what keeps her from being an unattainable, workaholic superwoman is the grand finale in verse 30: "Charm is deceptive, and beauty is fleeting; but a woman who fears the LORD is to be praised."

This idea of fearing the Lord can be easily misunderstood. I've heard people ask skeptically, "Why would we serve a God who wants us to fear Him?" That couldn't be further from the truth. In fact, we serve a God who loves us and wants to be loved in return. And we know there is no fear in love.

The problem comes when we define the word *fear* as dread. But it has multiple definitions, and the Hebrew word used here means "reverence" and "worship." What a different picture we get when our devotion to the Lord is what matters most.

Generations of women have gotten discouraged reading Proverbs 31. Maybe they missed verse 30 as the key to unlocking everything leading up to it. But that was surely not the intent of the poet. I imagine the end of the poem was intended to leave the reader with one grand, lasting impression: the fear of the Lord should be the foundation of our lives.

It's also important to read the juxtaposition in that verse, as the author identifies what won't last: external efforts and beauty.

As we look at the work we face today, whether that's caring for children, running a home-based business, or working outside the home, this principle will change our perspective. When we reverence and worship the Lord Almighty first and foremost, our priorities change. He becomes our "boss."

A woman who fears the Lord will honor His commands. And as we will see, God's commands do not include working ourselves to exhaustion. This ideal woman would have prayed, obeyed God's instruction, and honored the Sabbath. She would have guarded her time with God.

The next lesson comes from God Himself.

Do Only a Few Important Things Every Day

Just like God could have made the Garden of Eden self-sustaining, He also could have created the world in one day. One breath, one word, one sweep of the hand would have done it. Instead, God spread out creation over six days.

Whether you believe it was a literal six days or not, the principle is the same: God focused His attention on a few things each day.

This is a principle that has deeply impacted me over the years. Before I learned it, my to-do list might have included twenty or more things that I couldn't possibly do in a day. Maybe I'd check off a few things, always feeling like a failure because of how much was left on the list.

God modeled a simplicity of work that feels refreshing and focused.

Compare that to the Creator of the universe, who chose to model only a few accomplishments a day. Let's review the days of creation:

Day 1   God created light and separated it from the darkness. He called it "day" and "night."

Day 2   God created the sky.

Day 3   God created dry ground. He called it "land," and He called the water "seas." He also created vegetation.

Day 4   God created the sun, moon, and stars to give light to the earth.

Day 5   God created living creatures in the water and sky.

Day 6   God created living creatures on the land, including humankind.

God modeled a simplicity of work that feels refreshing and focused.

How might our approach to work change if we identified only a few key things to accomplish in a day? Of course, there are lots of little daily things we do, like making appointments or sending emails. But what if our to-do list only had a few things on it? This is possible, and if you keep reading, I'll explain how to do this in a later chapter.

Home Is Our First Line of Ministry

As we move through Scripture into the New Testament, we find the first translations that use the word *busy*. Surprisingly, busy is connected with women and their homes, and it is described in a positive light.

The first reference that translates the original word as "busy" is in Titus 2:3–5:

> Likewise, teach the older women to be reverent in the way they live, not to be slanderers or addicted to much wine, but to teach what is good. Then they can urge the younger women to love their husbands and children, to be self-controlled and pure, to be busy at home, to be kind, and to be subject to their husbands, so that no one will malign the word of God.

The word translated "busy" in this passage is the Greek word *oikourgos*, which means "to do work or labor in your home or dwelling place." It would seem being busy had a high value, specifically for women. In fact, we are to teach others to be busy, especially at home.

As a career-minded young woman, I never understood the importance of caring for my home. Well, I understood the importance of keeping it clean and organized—not that mine was back then—because my mother kept a well-maintained home, so I was trained to do that.

But I didn't understand the holy calling of my home being a place of ministry. Rather, I prided myself on how much I did *outside* my home.

You might know the passage of Scripture where Paul lists his credentials for putting confidence in the "flesh"—in other words, in himself. He presents his résumé to the church at

Philippi basically to say, "If I can't put my confidence in this, who can?"

> If someone else thinks they have reasons to put confidence in the flesh, I have more: circumcised on the eighth day, of the people of Israel, of the tribe of Benjamin, a Hebrew of Hebrews; in regard to the law, a Pharisee; as for zeal, persecuting the church; as for righteousness based on the law, faultless. (Phil. 3:4–6)

I often think about that passage when I consider my personal résumé of overcommitment. I might say something like, "If anyone regrets being overbusy, I have more to regret than all of you."

You've already heard some of my story, but here's a snapshot: after having three boys within five years, I continued to colead women's ministry, sing in the choir at the traditional service and colead worship at the contemporary service, volunteer on the evangelism committee, teach Sunday school, direct children's ministry, colead vacation Bible school, be part of a small group Bible study, and work part-time outside the home.

My life was a mess. I desperately wanted to prove to myself and others that I could manage being a mom and doing it all. And that sense of responsibility I mentioned earlier made me just about lose my mind trying.

Those three little boys paid the highest price, with a mom who hissed at them to sit still, rushed them through their daily activities, and yelled out of frustration as my oh-so-in-control life crumbled around me.

It wasn't until I connected with Proverbs 31 Ministries that I even heard the idea of my home being my first line of ministry. I always thought ministry was what I did at church!

Ministry was not the daily act of washing clothes, making meals, tucking little ones in at night, and supporting my husband. Those tasks took a backseat to my "calling" to sing, lead, or teach at church.

I wish I could wind back time and relive those years with the heart and perspective I have now. What a difference it makes when you see your home as a place of ministry . . . your first and highest calling.

I'm all for women being obedient to God's call on their lives, and sometimes that means working outside the home. Even the Proverbs 31 woman modeled this as she took her goods to market. But what we discover *How we care for and* in Scripture, and what I've confirmed *use the homes God* through practical experience, is that *gives us matters.* my life is more peaceful and balanced when I prioritize family and home.

Maybe you're reading this and you aren't married or don't have children. I believe this principle of our homes being a place of ministry applies to all of us. How we care for and use the homes God gives us matters.

Every woman can use her home to make others feel welcome, bless others through meals, or create a place of prayer. With this perspective, even the mundane, daily tasks have more value.

All Work Has Value because We Are Serving Jesus

The fourth principle God has taught me about work is to give my best effort no matter what I'm doing. This isn't because God wants perfection. Rather, God wants our motives to be right. And when our motives are right, we are more likely to have a healthy relationship with work.

The Bible is full of admonitions to be productive and hardworking. But it's in the book of Colossians where the apostle Paul puts it all in perspective and gives our hearts marching orders.

Paul wrote to the believers in Colosse, who consisted of men and women from all walks of life, including slaves. It was specifically to those slaves that Paul gave this word: "Whatever you do, work at it with all your heart, as working for the Lord, not for human masters, since you know that you will receive an inheritance from the Lord as a reward. It is the Lord Christ you are serving" (Col. 3:23–24).

All work has value today when we imagine doing it for Jesus.

Not only were those slaves likely responsible for the lowliest of tasks, but they were doing it against their will and with no hope of relief. In the midst of this undesirable situation, Paul reminds them that their work has value because they are working for Jesus. What an amazing paradigm shift!

All work has value today when we imagine doing it for Jesus. When I take this viewpoint, I want to do my best. This means making sure I have the time and energy to do just that. When I'm overbusy, my work always suffers.

Work is truly God's gift to us. He designed us for it. He assigns us to it. He refines us through it. As we continue this discussion of how to do busy better, it's good to remember that work and being busy aren't the enemy. We have an enemy, and he wants to spoil what God meant for good.

Which means our enemy is also out to steal God's gift of rest from us. In the next chapter, we'll take a look at this gift as we discover rest was meant to be more than an afternoon nap or a Saturday at the park.

Five

God's Gift of Rest

My eighteen-month-old son was exhausted. I'd pushed him past nap time in order to finish my errands. And now making that last stop at the grocery store didn't seem worth it based on the meltdown that happened in aisle five.

We were finally home, but my little guy was miserable. He needed to sleep, but his crib was the last place he wanted to be. His sobs broke my heart as I bounced and rocked and tried to cuddle an inconsolable toddler. There was no comforting him until exhaustion took over and he finally slept.

Every mom knows the frustration of an overtired child. We know if they would only quit fussing they would get the rest they need. Yet they resist it with every ounce of their toddler might. Why would they fight what they need most of all?

I wonder if they fear giving up control. Perhaps as they grasp for independence, like learning to say "No" and "Mine," the thought of releasing themselves to sleep seems like a step back. They'd rather be pushing themselves to do all those things they are learning to do—walking, climbing, and basically scaring their moms, who wonder why they were so excited for this phase of development.

Isn't it interesting that decades past toddlerhood, we still resist rest? We push ourselves until we are overtired and then push ourselves some more.

Maybe we don't scream like we did when our moms tried to make us take naps, but we sure make ourselves (and others) miserable.

In the last chapter, I introduced the idea that God established a pattern of work and rest at creation. I hope you got a good sense of God's heart for work and how it was never meant to control our lives. As we've seen, sin has warped all of God's gifts. Consequently, rather than work being a blessing, it has burdened us to the point of exhaustion.

In this chapter, I'd like to take a look at God's gift of rest. This is the key we need to unlock this healthy symmetry between work and rest. Without rest in its right proportion, we will always feel out of sync.

I've always struggled with the idea of rest. I know I'm supposed to rest, but for so many years I resisted it, until in my mind, rest equaled exhaustion. I've asked questions like: Is hiking or swimming actually resting? Or am I only resting when I'm sitting reading a book or watching TV? And when the kids were small, going to church on Sunday seemed like the *opposite* of resting.

Some people can nap, and they swear by it. Just take a five-minute "power nap" they advise. Companies are installing nap pods for employees, airlines are putting them in airports, and you can even buy a portable napping pillow that encloses your entire head except for your nose and mouth.

Napping has the opposite effect on me. No matter how tired I might be, the second I close my eyes, my mind starts running and I'm wide awake.

Even vacations weren't restful. As I mentioned earlier in the book, my husband is a lot like me. So vacations were time to pack as much activity in as possible. We even scheduled our daily activities on a spreadsheet.

Rest seemed like such a waste of time when there was so much to do, and it didn't even seem possible anyway.

This question of proper rest nagged at me until I decided it was just too complicated to figure out how to do it right. This "whatever" attitude also impacted my honoring the Sabbath. What did rest mean on the Sabbath? I knew it meant not to work, but was ironing working if I was watching a movie while I did it?

Rest is a command, a promise, a reward.

The Israelites obviously struggled with the idea of rest on the Sabbath too, because they established detailed rules to make sure they knew the boundaries of work and rest. The *Holman Illustrated Bible Dictionary* says, "Thirty-nine tasks were banned, such as tying or untying a knot."[3] They even identified how far one could walk on the Sabbath, which was two thousand cubits (about a half mile).

Why do we find it so hard to rest? I'm not sure, but it must frustrate God that we reject His gift of rest. Through the prophet Isaiah, He said, "This is what the Sovereign LORD, the Holy One of Israel, says: 'In repentance and rest is your salvation, in quietness and trust is your strength, but you would have none of it'" (Isa. 30:15).

God's heart must break when we work ourselves nonstop. If pleasing God is my desire (and it is), then I must understand God's purpose for rest and prioritize it more in my life, starting with understanding what the Bible says about rest.

The concept of rest begins in Genesis and spans Scripture. Rest is a command, a promise, a reward. It's more than just a physical break from work; rest also brings peace and protection. Then there is spiritual rest and the inheritance of rest. Let's start with the most common definition: physical rest.

The Physical Sense of Rest

The first evidence of physical rest comes from Genesis, and it's the most common definition of rest, meaning to cease from whatever you are doing.

The God who didn't *need* to rest *chose* to rest after creating the universe in six days. After doing all the work He intended to do, God stopped.

I love that God just stopped working when He'd done enough. So many times I think of one more adjustment, refinement, tweak that I can do to my project or task. Or I think of my long master to-do list and know there's more I could do. It's a perfectionist's nightmare, as it's hard to feel like anything is finished to my satisfaction.

For years I lived with an underlying sense that rest needed to be earned. Only when I'd gotten everything done, and done well, could I take a break. And if I rested before I'd deemed myself "worthy," then guilt would steal my rest.

However, rest is not earned; it is a gift. The only contingency is we must accept it as God designed it. If we twist it so it fits our definition of rest, it's really camouflaged work.

God knows the work opportunities are endless, which is why in Exodus 34:21 He made rest more than a gift. It became a command: "Six days you shall labor, but on the seventh day you shall rest; even during the plowing season and harvest you must rest."

Don't you just know those Israelites were trying to figure out a loophole around this commandment to rest? I can almost hear one of them saying, "That fruit won't pick itself!" But even during the busiest seasons of the year, when they probably felt like they couldn't afford to rest, the Israelites most needed to rest.

Rest is not earned; it is a gift.

Of course, this is logical when we admit it to ourselves. When we are expending the most amount of energy, we most need to rest. But oh, how we fight it, thinking we can muscle through.

There's a lot we can push through, but not rest. God designed the need for rest—both physical and mental—into our bodies. We can push through pain and discomfort for months or years, but we'll need rest before we'll need food. The longest period a human has stayed awake is eleven days,[4] but the longest recorded duration without food is just over two months.[5]

Rest, whether it's taking a short break from labor or getting a good night's sleep, restores our physical strength and cognitive functions, both of which progressively diminish without rest. Eventually our bodies will shut down without our say.

When we acknowledge that rest makes us stronger and sharper mentally, rest doesn't seem counterproductive at all. Rather, it's one of the wisest choices we can make.

There is another sense of rest we find in the Bible, and that is spiritual rest. And this is where God wants physical rest to lead us.

The Spiritual Sense of Rest

Spiritual rest doesn't just happen when we cease working; it happens when we cease striving.

We stop striving to earn peace with God through our actions.

We stop striving to solve our own problems.

We stop striving to find wisdom in ourselves.

We stop striving to meet our own need for significance.

Spiritual rest is a deep sense of confidence that no matter what comes our way, God is still on the throne, He has not forgotten us, and He is working on our behalf.

This is the level of rest we too-busy women need to experience. We know we can stop working for a time, but that doesn't mean our striving stops. This striving is what keeps us from being fully present with others. It's what keeps us from receiving the full benefit of physical rest, and sadly, it limits our relationship with God.

God invites us to trust Him—really, really trust Him. He's not just a book of rules; He's a God who desires a relationship with us, but one that is based on trust.

The Israelites were promised this peace and rest, but they never received it due to their unbelief and hard-heartedness. So they constantly strived to get to the place of rest by establishing an intricate web of rules. If these rules were kept, then they would be at peace with God. Then they would be accepted. They felt they had to earn rest too.

All this changed when Jesus gave up His rights and offered Himself as a perfect sacrifice for our sins. Through faith in Jesus Christ, we have reconciliation and peace with God.

In Christ, the promise of spiritual rest is fulfilled.

Jesus said in Matthew 11:29, "Take my yoke upon you and learn from me, for I am gentle and humble in heart, and you will find rest for your souls." Jesus wasn't offering rest from work. He was offering rest that would keep us from overworking: rest for our souls. This idea of soul rest is so important I've dedicated an entire chapter of this book to it. For now, know that deep soul rest is possible.

Oh, how my soul stirs at the invitation of Jesus. This is the rest my soul longs for; it's what I was made for. To know with certainty I am loved, cared for, and protected. Not just on this earth but for eternity. This knowledge gives my soul an anchor and quiets the striving, relentless part of me that seeks security.

Although spiritual rest is a gift, I would be remiss if I didn't mention we have a responsibility in all of this.

In Obedience Is Our Rest Confirmed

One of the hardest parts of being a parent is watching your child disobey and suffer the consequences. Every good parent knows their child's life would be so much easier if they'd just obey instructions.

Being a parent gives you the benefit of years of making your own mistakes. Basically, I could see danger when my children couldn't. And I knew that if they followed the rules my husband and I set, they would be protected from much harm.

Since God is the perfect parent, His rules go beyond our limited human ones. I can try to protect my kids physically and emotionally, but God knows what's best for our souls.

To fully experience God's spiritual rest—to experience the full range of His protection—we must lay down our will and choose to follow His. The Israelites did not learn this lesson in time.

After God freed the Israelites (we'll discuss this more in chapter 9), He led them to the Promised Land where they would find this kind of spiritual rest. But their disobedience and unbelief kept them from it—both from the rest and from entering the Promised Land.

The author of Hebrews speaks of the promise of this spiritual rest for the first believers and for us today. First, in chapter 3 we are warned not to harden our hearts toward God:

> Today, if you hear his voice,
>   do not harden your hearts
> as you did in the rebellion,
>   during the time of testing in the wilderness,
> where your ancestors tested and tried me,
>   though for forty years they saw what I did.
> That is why I was angry with that generation;
>   I said, "Their hearts are always going astray,
>   and they have not known my ways."
> So I declared on oath in my anger,
>   "They shall never enter my rest." (Heb. 3:7–11)

Then, in chapter 4, we are offered this good news:

Therefore, since the promise of entering his rest still stands, let us be careful that none of you be found to have fallen short of it. For we also have had the good news proclaimed to us, just as they did; but the message they heard was of no value to them, because they did not share the faith of those who obeyed. Now we who have believed enter that rest. (4:1–3)

Obedience is important to God, just as it would be to any good parent. And to fully receive His rest, we must choose to walk in His ways.

We find another promise of rest through obedience in Jeremiah 6. Here, the prophet Jeremiah pronounces a dire warning from the Lord unto the tribe of Judah. It speaks of their disobedience and resulting lack of rest:

This is what the LORD says:
    "Stand at the crossroads and look;
      ask for the ancient paths,
    ask where the good way is, and walk in it,
      and you will find rest for your souls.
    But you said, 'We will not walk in it.'" (Jer. 6:16)

The "good way" is easy to find. Not only do we have God's Word written down for us and the Holy Spirit inside us but we also have Jesus who said, "I am the way and the truth and the life. No one comes to the Father except through me" (John 14:6).

God's promise of spiritual rest is still available for us today, and that is very good news for our weary souls.

In concluding this chapter, I want to share the connection between physical and spiritual rest. Although they are different, they are connected.

The Synergy of Physical and Spiritual Rest

We can have physical rest for our bodies, and we can have spiritual rest for our souls. However, the best kind of rest is when those two are combined. We'll see that in the next chapter when we discuss the Sabbath, but there's a well-known story in the Gospel of Mark that illuminates God's rest in an interesting way.

In Mark 6, Jesus sent His disciples out by twos to teach and share the good news of God's kingdom. Mark 6:12–13 says, "They went out and preached that people should repent. They drove out many demons and anointed many sick people with oil and healed them."

Imagine their excitement to return to Jesus and share all they had learned. Verses 30–31 tell us, "The apostles gathered around Jesus and reported to him all they had done and taught. Then, because so many people were coming and going that they did not even have a chance to eat, he said to them, 'Come with me by yourselves to a quiet place and get some rest.'"

It seems very intentional that Jesus told the disciples to come with Him. He could have told them to go find some food or rest on their own, but He draws them to Himself. Jesus had the rest they needed, but it wasn't going to be the rest they expected.

I wonder if Jesus believed the disciples needed more than a physical break from work. Maybe they needed to reset their focus away from their work and onto Him. After such a successful time of ministry, it would have been easy for the disciples to feel puffed up in themselves and their abilities. After all, they'd sent demons packing and healed the sick. Maybe Jesus wanted them to remember where their power came from.

Instead of a physical break, the disciples were faced with more ministry needs. Jesus and the disciples got in a boat and were headed to a quiet place, but people saw them leaving and ran ahead of them to be on the other side of the lake when they hit the shore.

What happens next is one of the greatest miracles recorded in the Bible. In fact, other than the resurrection, it's the only miracle told in all four Gospels.

Luke tells us Jesus had compassion on the people, and rather than resting, He began to teach them late into the evening. And because Jesus had been headed to a "remote place," there was no one selling food.

Scripture tells us there were five thousand men gathered that day, and experts say there might have been another ten to fifteen thousand women and children. That's a lot of hungry, tired people.

The disciples wanted to send the people away to go buy food, but Jesus had another plan. "You give them something to eat," Jesus said (Mark 6:37).

Jesus was truly a master teacher. Not only did He teach the people who followed Him, but He had a lesson for His disciples as well.

If Jesus had been planning to reset the disciples' focus *away* from themselves and their abilities and *onto* Him, what better way than to assign them an impossible task? *That* would reset their minds very quickly toward who really had the power.

I can imagine myself standing there . . . just hours ago I'd been so proud of all I'd done. Now here I stand, completely helpless to do anything about the need before me. Maybe I even feel a bit foolish for getting all puffed up.

But Jesus didn't leave His disciples in that helpless place. He sent them to find what food they had, and they returned with five loaves of bread and two fish. Jesus looked to heaven, gave thanks, and broke the loaves. Then the disciples distributed those meager rations to the crowd, and after everyone had eaten, there were twelve baskets of bread and fish left over.

When Jesus invited the disciples to rest, I have to believe He knew this opportunity would arise. Maybe the rest the disciples needed that day was *spiritual rest*. Spiritual rest teaches us that God is our source, our portion, our provider. When we truly understand that, our souls sigh in relief.

If we deconstruct our lives and abilities, we know our power is frail. But God's power is infinite. Jesus always wants to reset our attention onto Him to give us this gift of spiritual rest. We experience it in prayer and worship. We experience it sitting quietly before Him. When we stop working long enough to rest, and turn our hearts and minds to Jesus, we remember our true source of power isn't ourselves.

I remember one particularly hectic school morning after getting all five kids out the door. I turned back to the kitchen and it was a disaster. There were papers strewn over every surface, a lunch box left on the counter from the day before, breakfast dishes everywhere, stray clothes, scattered shoes, blankets left on the couch, dog fur forming balls, and the list went on.

My heart felt overwhelmed. No matter how hard I worked to keep things in order, it felt like chaos was always trying to burst forth, much like trying to keep a beach ball underwater. In the midst of the chaos, I sensed Jesus inviting me to sit down for a minute.

But how could I? Back then I felt so strongly that my work had to be done before I could "treat" myself to some quiet time, especially since I worked at home. I had to have the dishes clean, counters cleared, urgent emails addressed, laundry going, etc. By the time I'd done all that, something else always demanded my attention, and my time with Jesus was neglected.

But not that day. That day I sat at the kitchen table and looked at my mess. It was big. I thought about the invitation to sit quietly with Jesus. I had to fight my instinct to get up, but I stayed put.

Satan knows that when we depend on our power, that's all the power we will see.

I sat in the middle of my mess and spent time with Jesus. I pictured Him sitting across the table from me. It was pure pleasure . . . and the mess amazingly faded from my view. My stress melted away, and I felt renewed. There was a joy I can't explain that stayed with me throughout the day.

Those few minutes of time have stuck in my mind for over ten years. In the midst of so much to do, I chose to rest, and the deep sense of peace and purpose God gave me sustained me to get up and go back to work.

That day I experienced the same rest God promised Moses in Exodus 33:14, "The LORD replied, 'My Presence will go with you, and I will give you rest.'"

God has done His best work in and through me when I have rested from my work and ceased striving to do things my way . . . when I have taken my hands off the steering wheel and let God lead.

This is a secret our enemy doesn't want us to know. He wants us to think that in rest we find weakness. Satan knows that when we depend on our power, that's all the power we will see.

But when we trust and believe in God's power, we will see amazing things happen. For those of us who resist rest, this is very good news.

Six

Four Conditions
of Unhealthy Busyness

For too many years I was too busy. Then I started learning what I've shared with you so far and made significant changes to balance my schedule.

I stepped out of volunteer positions, cut back my hours at work, and learned to honor the Sabbath. I still kept a productive pace, but this time healthier. Yet when people commented on how much I got done, there was this bit of shame that crept into my heart.

Were their observations innocent, or were they a veiled suggestion, with a hint of disapproval, that I still worked too much? Why did I still feel so guilty about my level of work?

Something has happened in certain Christian subcultures where being busy is akin to worshipping idols. There's an idea that living a slower-paced life should be everyone's goal.

And I certainly agree with *not* living life at breakneck speed. Been there, done that, have the scars to prove it.

But what if I'm just not wired to take it slow? There's not a day goes by that I don't thank God for the health He's given me. This is a blessing I want to steward well and not take one day for granted.

The problem with wiring like mine (and I imagine yours) is I get too busy. It's like there's a momentum that urges me on, until I find myself overloaded. Being busy isn't the problem. Being busy in an unhealthy way is.

In reviewing the times in my life when I've been on overload, I've discovered four conditions of unhealthy busyness: being busy without boundaries, being a busybody, doing work I'm not called to do, and focusing on busywork over my best work.

Being Busy without Boundaries

The most significant reason busy seems like the enemy is that we don't *stop* being busy often enough. We seamlessly move between jobs, housework, sports, church, service projects, volunteer positions, and family commitments with no downtime between.

We are busy all the time.

And when something consumes your life, it's easy to feel like you are battling an invisible enemy. Hence, "busy" becomes our adversary.

There have been so many times when I lived without a pause button, but one fall season ranks among the worst. All five of our children were in elementary school and involved in sports. The three boys played on three different football teams (due to age/weight restrictions), one daughter was a cheerleader, and the other daughter played soccer. If that wasn't enough, my husband owned and ran a consulting firm, I worked part-time and sang on the worship team, and my husband and I led a small group at church.

Our lives consisted of an ongoing handoff of children and responsibilities that needed military precision to keep them moving.

There was no time to meander, stroll, or take the scenic route. And there were literally no breaks. Days ran into nights and weeks blurred into months without us having any time to relax and catch our breath.

Thankfully it didn't last forever since the football season came to an end, but I declared *that* kind of overload would never, ever happen again. There was absolutely no margin for error or sickness.

What I realized in the aftermath was we had no nonnegotiable boundaries set in place to protect against that kind of crazy. Everything was fair game to cancel so we could get more done. We gave up on family dinners, evenings were filled with leftover work, there was no leisure time, and we didn't guard the Sabbath.

> *Unless I put borders around my busyness, I will be a wreck, and my family will too.*

That season, and many others before it, proved that unless I put borders around my busyness, I will be a wreck, and my family will too.

For most of us, there are few nonnegotiable boundaries when it comes to work. That's just the way our generation rolls. We live without the built-in rhythm of the rising and setting sun that guided our ancestors just a few generations back. Few of us live an agricultural or pastoral life led by the gentle demands of animals and crops.

We could work twenty-four hours a day if our bodies and minds would let us. Hence, we get drawn into a nonstop lifestyle of work.

Although I firmly believe the Bible honors hard work, the Bible *doesn't* say we need to be busy all the time. This is where we need wisdom to know when to work and when to stop. Jesus modeled rest as well as hard work. He knew when to draw away from the crowds, from ministry, from work, and when to press pause in the middle of the day. Jesus also modeled keeping the Sabbath as a complete day of rest and honor to God.

I love how King David acknowledges God's perfect plans: "Lord, you alone are my portion and my cup; you make my lot secure. The boundary lines have fallen for me in pleasant places; surely I have a delightful inheritance" (Ps. 16:5–6).

God has boundary lines established for our lives that are pleasant and manageable. Although David refers to property lines, this is a lovely image of how God doesn't plan to give us chronic overcommitment. Just as there are boundaries for property, we need boundaries on our time and commitments. Without boundaries, we will sacrifice the important for the urgent.

At the edge of every boundary there needs to be margin. Every city has different rules for this, but you probably know you can't build your house right on your property line. You have to move it back a certain number of feet. This creates a margin for safety.

This is true in property boundaries and it's also true in graphic design. Margin, or white space, allows breathing room and balance for the eye and mind—both in design and in our lives.

I learned this concept back in college when I took an editing class required for my journalism degree. As editors, we had to learn everything about a well-designed page of content. From the size of the headlines, to the number of columns, to the placement of ads, it was an editor's job to work with the typesetter to make sure the page was easy to read. Hard to believe we still had typesetters back then—and I don't mean the Gutenberg kind, lest you think I'm a few hundred years old.

While I don't remember most of what I learned in that class, I vividly remember the importance of white space. I learned the beauty of design isn't just what you see, it's what you don't see. It's sometimes called the "negative space," and the undesigned space carries as much, if not more, impact as the words or graphics.

Just as white space adds beauty to any piece of art, the printed page, a website or ad, white space in our lives serves a similar benefit.

Artists and designers strategically use white space to serve a number of purposes. And as we consider the idea of putting boundaries around our busyness, white space can serve a purpose for us as well.

One significant value of white space is to make the page visually appealing so you want to read it. This is one reason we see shorter paragraphs in all kinds of copy. As our eyes scan a crowded page, our minds tell us it's too much work, and we disengage.

But a piece with lots of white space invites you in. It doesn't feel overwhelming or chaotic. It feels simple, doable, calm. White space gives the reader a mental break while at the

By establishing boundaries for our busyness, we give ourselves breathing room.

same time drawing attention to the most important things on the page.

And this is what a life with white space does for us. When our lives are overcrowded with "content" and lacking white space, we will feel cluttered and confused. It's hard to identify what's most important because it all runs together in a blur.

But by establishing boundaries for our busyness, we give ourselves breathing room. We give ourselves time to think, time to dream, and time to plan. Busy gets seriously out of control without boundaries.

Being a Busybody

The next problem with busyness is found in 2 Thessalonians 3:11: "We hear that some among you are idle and disruptive. They are not busy; they are busybodies."

In this chapter of the Bible, busy is not a problem; in fact, it's the ideal. The problem is idleness, the opposite of busyness.

It seems the problem facing this young Thessalonian church was a small group of members who weren't doing their share of the work. Their actions led to distraction for those who were working. This idleness was such a problem that Paul (the author of 2 Thessalonians) told them to keep away from this group of troublemakers.

In a play on words, Paul calls the idle group "busybodies." A busybody can look busy, but in reality they are busy with things that don't concern them. As a result, they neglect the work they should be doing.

The word *busybodies* is translated from the Greek word *periergazomai*, meaning "a meddler." This is someone who gets herself caught up in the business of others. In other words, she's busy with work that is not hers to do.

As I consider this principle, it's so easy to see how we can fall into the same trap. I find myself constantly wanting to get involved in the business of others to the neglect of my own work. Just this past week we had a problem in another department at work, and I had an idea on how to solve it. I wanted to step in and offer my help.

Sometimes that's the right thing to do. But in reality, they didn't need my help to solve the problem. They had competent people who would come up with a good solution. I caught myself before I overstepped my position and redirected my attention to what was on my agenda.

In our world of social media and entertainment, it's so easy to get over-involved in the business of others to the neglect of our own business. Whether it's scrolling through posts, reading magazines, or watching entertainment news, we are fascinated with the lives of others.

When their lives seem more interesting or exciting than ours, we start comparing ourselves to them and becoming discontent with our own lives. Then, rather than working to improve our own situation, we find it easier and more pleasant to stay focused on theirs.

I wonder how much more productive we'd be if we took the time we spent on the business of others and applied it to our own work. It's a question worth pursuing.

I'm Not Called to Do What I'm Doing

Another problem that leads to being overbusy is when I assume responsibilities that I'm not called to assume. When that happens, I'm ineffective in what I *am* called to do, and I end up once again with a chaotic schedule.

This question of what God is calling me to do takes some internal wrestling. I wish it were as easy as the *Sesame Street* game "One of these things is not like the other . . ." Then I could look at five things on my plate and remove one. But normally it takes more prayer and consideration than that.

My life can be filled with responsibilities that look good; in fact, they *are* good. But they may not be *my* good.

Capable women find themselves overcommitted in these places all the time. For example, how many times have you sat in a meeting where the leader of the group, department, or ministry presents a need and then looks to the unenthusiastic crowd for someone to step up and take on this important role?

[Enter the sound of crickets while people look at their phones or pretend to write something down.]

Someone, usually me, can't stand the quiet any longer and raises her hand.

And so it goes. Once again I've stepped up because I thought no one else would. Maybe they would have if I hadn't jumped in. Or maybe, truth be told, I like coming to the rescue . . . being the responsible one . . . being needed.

However, if those are my reasons for saying yes, I'm actually walking in disobedience. What I've learned the hard way is to build in a cushion of prayer before taking on a new responsibility. Allowing for time is as simple as saying, "May I have time to pray about this?" If you aren't in a situation where it's comfortable to say "pray," then just say, "May I have time to consider this?"

If the answer is no, then that's probably your answer too. Unless God has clearly told me in advance to say yes,

I've never had to give an answer based on someone else's timetable.

Our good intentions can lead us down paths that cause complications for us and remove opportunities for others. Author Kristine Brown wrote about this very thing in her *Encouragement for Today* devotion titled "When Good Intentions Get in the Way."

Kristine told about stepping up to help coach her daughter's soccer team when it seemed no one else would. The season was a discouraging series of losses, despite Kristine's valiant attempts to learn the sport of soccer after only taking dance lessons as a child.

As grateful as I am for grace, my hope is to listen well before I raise my hand.

At the end of the season, another parent came up to Kristine and asked, "How did you get involved in coaching? This is something I would really enjoy doing!"

Kristine summed up the experience well:

> We work with such enthusiasm, don't we? We try our best to love, help and give. In our zeal, sometimes we step into places God never intended for us. Just like a flower-picking ballerina attempting to coach little-league soccer. But God knows us so well, and He offers grace when we get ahead of Him. . . .
>
> He [the other parent] could have been the next person on the list of potential volunteers, but my good intentions got in the way. *Lord, forgive me.*[6]

I love her take on this common issue. Even when we get ourselves into a place we haven't been called, God offers us grace. As grateful as I am for grace, my hope is to listen well before I raise my hand.

Busywork or Our Best Work?

The last condition of unhealthy busyness is when I focus on busywork over my best work. Busywork used to mean a teacher giving kids a worksheet. Today busywork can look like work, but it's empty of value. Let me try to explain this with a food analogy.

I love empty calories. Chocolate brownies are my favorite. Although I try to tell myself the eggs inside make them healthy, the truth is there is little in that fudgy goodness that brings value to my body. Besides the moment of pleasure in my mouth, it only brings harm. It fulfills my body's need for calories but offers no nutrition.

Being busy can have the same effect. We can fill our days with busywork, then flop on the couch after dinner, exhausted. And yet we look around our homes and wonder why a week's worth of mail is stacked on the desk, dirty clothes drape over the hamper, and the kitchen floor is a slip and slide . . . but we were *so* busy!

Much like the woman who spends $100 at the grocery store and has nothing for dinner, if we aren't wise about our busyness, we will find ourselves frustrated at how little gets done. Like the brownies and their empty calories, there is activity that keeps us busy but produces little benefit.

One area of temptation to empty busyness is my computer. Because I'm an editor and writer, I spend a lot of my workday at the computer. If I sit down without a plan, two hours can pass and nothing is accomplished—except for watching videos of baby animals. However, when I take the time to set goals for my day, it's easy to stay focused.

The same is true for my housework. When I take a few minutes to identify my priorities for that day, the tasks that need to be accomplished get done. Otherwise, it's 7 p.m. and I'm wondering what's for dinner.

The Bible warns against idleness, as I pointed out earlier in the chapter, and we are no different from those early believers. Only our idleness looks different—it can look like busyness. In fact, we might even convince ourselves that it was necessary to get caught up on the news, visit a friend's blog, or research next year's vacation. Important? Yes. A priority for today? Maybe not.

Being aware of what constitutes busywork for me makes such a difference. When I catch myself answering emails rather than working on an important project, I shut down my email provider so I'm not distracted.

Also, if I have tasks I'd really rather not do, I force myself to do those first. I'm an expert procrastinator, so it's important for me to do my hard work first, or I'll get caught up in busywork and neglect my best work. I've also learned some tricks about managing my to-do list that I'll share in another chapter.

Busy isn't the enemy—or as I like to say, it's not a four-letter word. (Note the irony.)

My challenge is to be a good steward of my time—at work, play, and rest. Busy isn't always bad. Only when it's busy without boundaries and busy on the wrong things. And brownies aren't bad either. At the right time.

Seven

Hurry Is a Heart Condition

Most of us long for life to slow down. Perhaps that's why so many of us love to read about the Amish and earlier, simpler times. There's something so attractive about a lifestyle led by a simple faith, the sun, and seasons.

But I'll be honest, I'm not sure I could give up my electronic devices. In fact, I'm pretty sure I have a slight addiction to my laptop and smartphone. And by slight I mean significant.

And I am still waiting for my smartphone to make me smarter. Somehow I just feel dumber when I enter an appointment on my phone and it shows up on my computer—but not my phone. I can't figure it out. It's like they are in cahoots.

I think if we were all honest, we'd be miserable if things slowed down. We'd much rather things hurry up.

We hurry everything. Consider the following recent developments:

- Thirty-minute meals have been replaced by five-minute meals.
- There's a 3-in-1 shampoo, conditioner, and body wash created to cut your time showering.
- Ten-minute exercise programs have been designed for the impatient athlete.
- Emergency rooms now advertise their wait times on billboards along the freeway, just in case you get in an accident while you are distracted by looking at their amazingly quick service.
- Do you know which button on an elevator is pushed most? Close.

We are an impatient society. We *like* things fast.

And I'm no exception. I'm getting more and more impatient all the time. Some days it's like there is an internal stopwatch inside me. It's as if I'm on the starting line and someone yells, "Ready. Set. Go!" And the clock starts ticking.

When that happens, I walk fast, I work fast, and heaven help me if my internet connection takes longer than a few seconds to load a website. Of course, I have completely forgotten that I used to have a dial-up connection.

And the more I hurry, the more it seems I hit every red light and choose the longest line (even if it looks shortest). And for the life of me, I can't get in and out of a grocery store in under an hour—even if I go in for a few items.

Not only is my technology in cahoots, but sometimes it feels like there's a grand conspiracy to slow me down. I force myself to be patient with people, but I let it all hang out on gadgets that just won't do what I want them to do . . . NOW!

We should have lots of extra time with all this hurrying. But we don't! In fact, if I took a poll, I imagine you would all say you have less free time than five years ago. You know this same feeling of being in a hurry and having time fly by, like when you're trying to get a project done by deadline, get all your errands done on your day off, or feel like you're getting older and opportunities are slipping away. (And yet somehow, time still drags between meals when we're on a diet.)

Hurry is the enemy of what matters most in life.

We feel hurry in so many different situations. The problem is that hurry is the enemy of what matters most in life.

The Lord convicted me of my hurry problem years ago when I read John Ortberg's timeless book *The Life You've Always Wanted.*

Ortberg refers to what is known as "hurry sickness," and outlines the symptoms of this condition that afflicts so many of us overbusy women. In the opening of his chapter titled "An Unhurried Life," he tells this story of asking a wise man for advice:

> Not long after moving to Chicago, I called a wise friend to ask for some spiritual direction. I described the pace of life in my current ministry. The church where I serve tends to move at a fast clip. I also told him about our rhythms of family life: we are in the van-driving, soccer-league, piano-lesson, school-orientation-night years. I told him about the present condition of my heart, as best I could discern it. What did I need to do, I asked him, to be spiritually healthy?
>
> Long pause.
>
> "You must ruthlessly eliminate hurry from your life," he said at last.

Another long pause.

"Okay, I've written that one down," I told him, a little impatiently. "That's a good one. Now what else is there?" I had many things to do, and this was a long-distance call, so I was anxious to cram as many units of spiritual wisdom into the least amount of time possible.

Another long pause.

"There is nothing else," he said. "You must ruthlessly eliminate hurry from your life."[7]

I have discovered this lesson myself: hurry usually costs more than it gains. And of course, like most of the lessons in my life, I had to learn this the hard way, in the trenches and with regrets.

As Ortberg listed the symptoms of hurry sickness, I could check "yes" to every one. But the symptom that cut me to the quick was a diminished capacity to love.

I didn't have to look far in my past to confirm this was a problem. My rushed lifestyle didn't allow time for gentle characteristics of love outlined in Scripture. First Corinthians 13:4–7 describes love, and as you can see, my impatient personality strikes out right at the beginning:

> Love is patient, love is kind. It does not envy, it does not boast, it is not proud. It does not dishonor others, it is not self-seeking, it is not easily angered, it keeps no record of wrongs. Love does not delight in evil but rejoices with the truth. It always protects, always trusts, always hopes, always perseveres.

Hurry and love are incompatible. A hurried person is more concerned with their own agenda than with others every time.

To love others we must be fully present. That's when I feel most loved by others. When someone stops what they are doing and makes it clear there's no place they'd rather be than with me—it fills up my emotional love tank.

That's how I want others to feel about me. I want to be the one to stop and give my whole heart and mind to the person in front of me. I want them to know their thoughts, needs, and hurts have 100 percent of my attention.

People can sense when you are in a hurry, because hurry slips out in our tapping toes, rapping fingertips, and distracted eyes. Hurried people are tightly wound and can give off the impression there is *somewhere* else to be or *someone* more important to be with at that moment. We've all gotten that impression from a friend, coworker, or church leader, and it leaves us feeling less-than.

God's to-do list always involves loving others fully, being patient, and only doing the things He assigns me to do.

Another lesson I've learned is that hurry isn't connected with *what* I am doing. I can be at work, on the road, at church, or at home. Hurry is not a required by-product of any one kind of lifestyle. A homeschooling mom can be more hurried than an executive. A retired person can be more hurried than a working mom of five. It doesn't matter whether I am a leader, student, teacher, truck driver, or missionary: hurry is a heart condition.

The only people who have a good excuse to hurry are those heroes of our nation who serve in emergency situations. For the rest of us, in 99 percent of all our life situations, we need to ruthlessly eliminate hurry.

As I've dissected the most rushed times of my life, even though there might be exceptions, hurry was the result of following my to-do list rather than God's assignments for my life.

My to-do list and God's to-do list aren't always the same. God's to-do list always involves loving others fully, being patient, and only doing the things He assigns me to do.

The most chaotic times for me were when I was in the driver's seat of my life. There were years as a Christian that I *never* thought about asking God's direction for me.

Of course I would go to college.

Of course I would pursue a career.

Of course we would have kids.

Of course I would help lead women's ministry.

Of course I would direct children's ministry.

I just piled on responsibility after responsibility because they were all good things! And of course God wants me to do good things, right? I overloaded my life and was in constant hurry mode to get it all done. The perfect example of this was on a return trip from family vacation.

Do you remember *The Beverly Hillbillies* television show? The intro set the scene for this backwoods family, with all their possessions piled up and tied on the back of their flatbed truck. That's what my family looked like while heading to the airport after a week of vacation.

We should have anticipated the line to return the rental car, but we didn't. So minutes ticked away as we sat in line, inching toward the front. We hadn't allowed for this extra time, and we got increasingly anxious as it looked like we weren't going to make our flight.

Once we finally got the car returned, we decided to run for it. Before I tell you the rest of the story, I should mention that our three children at the time were seven, five, and three. And the littlest, Robbie, had fractured a bone in his foot during our stay and was in a tiny blue orthopedic boot.

So we crammed suitcases, backpacks, and tote bags on a luggage cart and raced (as best we could with three boys, one with a broken foot) to the ticket counter.

Only we overloaded the cart. Every few steps something started slipping. My husband was pushing and I was pulling, both of us trying to balance the overloaded cart. We thought we were managing decently, even with our stops and starts, until we approached the elevator.

Our oldest, Josh, went ahead to hold the elevator door open. But as we went up the sloped curb, bags started slipping, and within seconds everything fell apart.

Robbie stopped in front of the cart for some reason. My husband didn't see him as he reached for a slipping bag, and he ran over Robbie's foot. Robbie screamed, my husband yelled for help with the bags, and at that exact moment the elevator started beeping in objection to being held open for so long and Josh began crying in fear.

In seconds, we were in a total meltdown, and there was no loving patience demonstrated.

If only we had left our hotel with lots of extra time. If only we had anticipated the wait at the rental car return. If only we hadn't overloaded the cart. If only we hadn't gotten frustrated with scared and hurt children. If only . . .

I wish I could say those types of experiences were exceptions, but during that time in my life I was always trying to do one last thing before leaving the house, trying to fit one more errand into an already busy afternoon, or taking on much more than I could handle. The result? Hurry.

My responsibilities outweighed my capacity to manage them. Every day was an exercise in frustration—with myself, my home, my husband, and my children.

Why couldn't anyone get it together?

Why didn't the demands stop?

Why did everyone *need* me so much?

I even got annoyed at the dentist's office when I was rushing to an appointment . . . as if it was their fault my children's teeth needed a cleaning.

Hurry made me feel like a victim! But I wasn't.

When we hurry, we miss what God has put right in front of us. God has not promised us tomorrow. Oh, there will be a tomorrow. But we aren't guaranteed to have it. Which is the paradox and why I feel a sense of hurry.

Hurry Is Not the Same as Busy

Hopefully by now I've convinced you that busy doesn't have to be bad. It is possible to be busy in a healthy, productive way.

Jesus had to be busy. How else did He get so much done in three years? But we never read of Jesus being in a hurry.

Jesus's pace would probably drive some of us nuts. At times He pushed through being tired and hungry to minister to someone in need. The story of the woman at the well is a perfect example.

In John 4, Jesus and His disciples were traveling north to Galilee, and they passed through Samaria. I'm pretty sure the disciples wanted to hurry through this area, because Jews didn't associate with Samaritans.

But Jesus had other plans. As they approached the city of Sychar in the middle of the day, Jesus stopped by a well to rest while the disciples went to purchase food. As He waited, a solitary woman came to draw water, and Jesus engaged her in a life-changing conversation—not only for her but for her entire village.

On this day, Jesus could have pleaded exhaustion or frustration. He'd been traveling, it was warm, and He was hungry. Just one of those challenges would have been enough to keep me hurrying to get the day over with rather than ministering to someone's deepest need.

Instead, Jesus narrowed His focus on one woman and finished the assignment God gave Him.

After Jesus reunited with His disciples, they tried to get Him to eat. He responded, "My food . . . is to do the will of him who sent me and to finish his work" (John 4:34).

Jesus always followed His Father's to-do list, which included times of productivity and times of rest. But in spite of all there was to do, Jesus was never hurried. He could not be rushed by the demands of others.

He stopped to care for children and those crippled at birth. He stopped in a crowd when someone touched His cloak. And the Scriptures tell us Jesus often withdrew from people in order to spend time alone with God. Luke 5:15–16 says, "The news about him spread all the more, so that crowds of people came to hear him and to be healed of their sicknesses. But Jesus often withdrew to lonely places and prayed." And Mark writes, "Very early in the morning, while it was still dark, Jesus got up, left the house and went off to a solitary place, where he prayed. Simon and his companions went to look for him, and when they found him, they exclaimed: 'Everyone is looking for you!'" (Mark 1:35–37).

One of the striking things about these passages is the fact that Jesus withdrew from the crowds just when He was most in demand. There were thousands, perhaps tens of thousands, of people waiting for Jesus to heal them, to teach them, to bless them. They were primed. They were ready. The opportunity was great. The need was great. And yet, Jesus was nowhere to be found.

Why? Wasn't that irresponsible, to take a day off when there were so many people needing His help? Wasn't that a bit self-indulgent? Not in the least. Jesus understood that the need was endless. But in order to accomplish the purpose for which God had sent Him, He had to remain spiritually strong. And that required regular times of prayer and meditation, regular times of rest and recuperation.

Jesus did not demand or desire that His followers hustle and hurry to the point of exhaustion and burnout. He knew they needed periods of rest in order to remain strong, just as we do.

In John 5:19, Jesus confirmed His unrushed to-do list with these words: "Very truly I tell you, the Son can do nothing by himself; he can do only what he sees his Father doing, because whatever the Father does the Son also does."

Jesus is really our model for an unhurried life. Productive but peaceful. Passionate about God's plans, but not at the expense of people.

We will always get into trouble when we take our eyes off Jesus. Even the most well-meaning, brightest, and humanly best experts in time management can't come close to the wisdom of following God's plan for our lives.

It defies human logic, but it's His best for our best, because only God knows how He designed us to work.

For example, if I tried to use a typewriter like a computer, I would constantly be disappointed in the typewriter. I would be annoyed that I had to pick up my hand from the keys to slide the return bar at the end of every line. I would get frustrated every time I had to find Wite-Out to paint over a mistake. Or use carbon paper to make a duplicate copy.

Hurry robs us of the beauty God has placed in front of us and the grace that others so desperately need.

A typewriter can't come close to working like a computer.

We are a little like a typewriter. God didn't design us with a ridiculous amount of memory, or the ability to press a delete button when we make a mistake, or a mind that processes an uncountable number of thoughts at once and sorts them in order of relevance.

We were designed to go at a slower pace, to ponder, to process thoughts one at a time. And when we try to go at computer speed, we miss out on what's important in life.

Hurry robs us of the beauty God has placed in front of us and the grace that others so desperately need. Hurry is also a tool Satan uses to undermine God's plan for us.

Satan Uses Hurry

I've mentioned a few times so far that we have an enemy. The Bible refers to him as the devil or by his given name, Satan. This enemy is found throughout Scripture, from Genesis, where we meet him as the serpent who deceived Eve, to Revelation, where his doom is predicted.

Jesus called him a "thief" and warned that he's out to steal and destroy everything good in our lives. In John 10:9–11, Jesus says,

> I am the gate; whoever enters through me will be saved. They will come in and go out, and find pasture. The thief comes only to steal and kill and destroy; I have come that they may have life, and have it to the full. I am the good shepherd. The good shepherd lays down his life for the sheep.

Using hurry as a tool, here are some of the things Satan steals.

Our Right Response

Hurry leads us to jump to conclusions. When I'm in a hurry, I don't have time to hear someone out. I don't take time to pray about a response to someone who has offended me.

Hurry keeps me from being able to think deeply about a situation and come up with the right response. Without fail, I've regretted a too-quick response every time. And many times I've set a bad situation in motion because of my rush to respond.

John 8 tells of a time when Jesus controlled the situation by pausing rather than responding immediately. He intentionally slowed the situation so people could think.

A woman had been caught in adultery and was brought before Jesus while He was teaching in the temple court. Imagine her shame as the Pharisees stood around pointing at her, demanding Jesus confirm their desire to stone her.

I can sense the frenzy of the mob mentality. But rather than giving His opinion and feeding their fury, Jesus bent down and started to write on the ground with His finger. His pause bought time . . . enough time for passions to cool, reason to return, and hearts to be prepared for His answer. Finally, Jesus stood and said, "Let any one of you who is without sin be the first to throw a stone at her" (John 8:7).

The only one who can hurry us to make a decision, form a judgment, or speak our opinion in any situation is us. This principle guides me to wait before sending an email, to pause before speaking my thoughts. Time helps me calm down and see things from another's perspective.

> *The only one who can hurry us to make a decision, form a judgment, or speak our opinion in any situation is us.*

Our Ability to Be Excellent

The story is told of two woodsmen, one of whom challenged the other to an all-day tree chopping contest. The challenger worked very hard, stopping only for a brief lunch break. The other man had a leisurely lunch and took several breaks during the day. At the end of the day, the challenger was surprised and annoyed to find that the other fellow had chopped substantially more wood than he had.

"I don't get it," he said. "Every time I checked, you were taking a rest, yet you chopped more wood than I did."

"But you didn't notice," said the winning woodsman, "that I was sharpening my ax when I sat down to rest."

This story reminds me of the power of taking my time to do something right . . . the first time. But oh, how I want to rush to get things done.

My youngest son worked in a kitchen for his first job, and was always coming home with burns and cuts on his hands. I knew he wanted to make a good impression on his bosses and was convinced that his knife speed would accomplish that. I later spoke with his manager (who was a friend of ours), and she told me he'd do much better if he'd only slow down.

Rushing doesn't make me better at anything. Unless it's athletics or speed eating, hurry doesn't guarantee success.

So many of us long to be excellent at something but chafe at the time it takes. If we could slow down, I wonder how the quality of our work would improve.

Our Contentment

Finally, hurry steals my contentment. As someone who struggles with her weight, I'm always looking for a tip to help me lose a few pounds. One tip is to eat slowly.

WebMD reports that it takes twenty minutes from the time we start eating for the brain to tell the stomach it's full.[8] Until then, we will keep eating in order to experience that sensation of being full. And in that time, we will overeat.

What a profound parallel to our need for speed in other areas of our lives. Could slowing down give us the time to feel content with what we have?

When I'm in a hurry, I don't appreciate the beauty around me. My awareness of others is diminished in my increased focus on the goal. I miss the small details of life that bring me the most joy in my rush.

Contentment isn't found in the big splashes but in the gentle ripples.

Hurry isn't our friend in the most important areas of life. Neither relationships, nor quality, nor depth can be found when we hurry. So the next time we feel that panic start to sneak in and push our gas pedal, let's pause and scribble in the sand, or whatever we need to do to slow ourselves down and regain control.

Eight

A Heart at Rest

If hurry is an attitude of the heart—and I believe it is—then we need to address what's going on in the depth of our heart that pushes us to rush rather than taking our time.

Years ago, a dear friend began a conversation with me this way: "I'm so sorry to bother you. I know how busy you are . . ." Everything in me wanted to contradict her, to reassure her that I was never too busy for her and that no matter what else was on my agenda, I would make time for her. I tried, but my life spoke the truth.

My friend saw the external proof of my internal reality. She saw how rushed I was and concluded I was too busy for her problem. Thankfully, she said something, but I wonder how many other people didn't say anything, silently writing me off as too busy to be a friend, too busy to help, too busy to care.

After that I made a decision to slow down in public. To walk slower, talk slower. To stop talking about all the work

I had to do, and to try and focus more on the person in front of me rather than the next item on my to-do list.

As with so many other times in my life, the Lord prompted me to do a heart search and get to the bottom of what drove me to hurry. In doing so, He revealed two issues that needed to be addressed.

I Must Seek God before Goals

Probably my biggest and saddest "aha" moment was realizing my desire to seek the satisfaction of completing a goal more than experiencing God.

This is a battle every morning, knowing my to-do list beckons. Tasks await, people expect, emails ding.

All the while my Bible sits on the table with a silent invitation. It's not demanding, simply offering a peaceful promise. Sadly, it's easy to pass as I move on to things I "need" to do.

I'm wired like Martha; maybe you know her from the Bible. She was concerned about her to-do list too.

Luke 10 records a day when Martha was the hostess and Jesus was a guest. It's a very short story, but we know that Martha fussed at Jesus because her sister wasn't working hard enough. Rather than helping Martha fix the food, Mary was sitting and listening to Jesus.

Jesus loved both Mary and Martha. But in that moment, as the story records, Jesus was more delighted with Mary's heart to be with Him than Martha's heart to serve Him.

I can be a fusser too. Too busy with the details, too worried about planning for what's next, too preoccupied with my to-do list. I even worry about other people's to-do lists.

Yet, I want a heart that pursues God more than I pursue my goals. I want to long to spend time in Jesus's presence more than I long to spend time on my computer or phone. It's not that I don't love Jesus. I do. I've devoted my life to serving Him. I'm aware of His presence and talk to Him throughout the day.

But so did Martha. She loved Jesus. And I'm sure she loved having Him as a houseguest, where she could hear Him talk as she went about her daily tasks. Maybe she asked Him questions as she served Him lunch. Touched His shoulder as she walked by and picked up His plate.

But she didn't stop to sit at His feet. She didn't pause her preparation to give Him wholehearted attention.

Jesus so gently and lovingly corrected Martha and gave her advice on the right way to go about her work:

> "Martha, Martha," the Lord answered, "you are worried and upset about many things, but few things are needed—or indeed only one. Mary has chosen what is better, and it will not be taken away from her." (Luke 10:41–42)

Jesus loved Martha's heart of service, but He wanted her wholehearted devotion first.

This was a message Jesus consistently taught in His ministry. Get your heart right first; that's the most important place to start. Jesus spoke these words to confirm this priority for our lives: "But seek first his kingdom and his righteousness, and all these things will be given to you as well" (Matt. 6:33).

I wonder if Martha changed her habits. Did she check her heart and consider where Jesus fit? Did she review her priorities and put Jesus before cleaning up?

We don't know the answer. The only thing we can know is what *we* decide to do with this story.

It's so compelling to jump into our days—whether it's fixing breakfast for children or leading a meeting at work—without ever pausing to sit at Jesus's feet. It's so much easier to whisper a prayer while driving carpool or listen to the Christian radio station and consider that our time with God.

God promises me a palace, and I settle for a shed when I seek my kingdom before His.

We can be sure that God loves to hear our prayers and songs of worship. But Martha's story challenges me to do a heart check: Why haven't I carved out time every day to just enjoy the presence of the Lord?

When Jesus said to seek God's kingdom first, this wasn't a one-and-done activity, at least not for me. Without an ongoing redirection of my priorities, I will tend toward seeking my own "kingdom" first.

This spiritual principle starts with a practical habit: press the pause button more often and check in with my heavenly Father. I need to ask for His wisdom in situations rather than depending on my own. And I need to ask for His Spirit to change my selfish wiring.

God promises me a palace, and I settle for a shed when I seek my kingdom before His.

Psalm 46:10 records the words of our Father on how to know Him: "Be still, and know that I am God." Funny that He didn't say, "Dive into your work and know that I am God."

Oh, that I would wake up with a burning desire to experience God's presence before ever thinking about a goal for the day!

I Must Choose People over Projects

The second heart problem God addressed with me is my tendency to choose projects over people.

In Matthew 22 the religious leaders asked Jesus about the greatest commandment. Jesus replied: "'Love the Lord your God with all your heart and with all your soul and with all your mind.' This is the first and greatest commandment. And the second is like it: 'Love your neighbor as yourself.' All the Law and the Prophets hang on these two commandments" (vv. 37–40).

I find it interesting that Jesus answered a question the Pharisees didn't ask. They only asked for the greatest commandment, not the second-greatest. But Jesus intertwined them. He obviously wanted His listeners to consider loving God and loving people as inseparable. But why?

Consider who Jesus was speaking to at the time. The Pharisees were religious leaders who insisted on the strict observance of Jewish law, and there were over six hundred commandments to follow: dietary laws, laws about clothing and hair care, laws about what you could and could not do on the Sabbath. These men were bound in legalism.

They were consumed with doing the right thing, which to them meant following the laws. And Jesus just told them the most important laws involved love: first God, then people. Perhaps Jesus knew we would tend toward one or the other.

We can love God and neglect loving people. Of course, none of us would admit that. But I've been guilty of serving God through my commitments at church, then getting annoyed with people and not showing compassion or God's kindness.

My tendency to put rules ahead of people was revealed a few years ago when I went with Compassion International to Quito, Ecuador. At that time it was a city of fifteen million people, with so many of those in desperate need of the love and help of Jesus and His followers.

The purpose of our tour was to experience Compassion International firsthand, then return home and write about the life-changing work they do in the lives of children and families. So we spent time in the project areas and even went into some homes.

One afternoon we split into groups with instructions to be back at the bus at 2:00 p.m. Our local guide ushered us into a home with a tin roof, blankets for walls, and dirt for the floor. The kindness of our hosts overshadowed the surroundings, and we spent an hour enjoying our time together.

But then it was time to go. We thanked the owners of the home, and the Americans in the group excused ourselves. However, our local guide remained. The rest of us stood outside as time ticked by—looking at our watches, then looking at each other with shrugs.

Two o'clock arrived and still we stood outside the little shack, waiting for our guide to finish visiting. We still had to trek to the bus.

Anxiety was mounting in our little group when one of the Americans who worked with Compassion turned to us and said, "The Ecuadorian people run their day by relationships, not the clock."

Ah, yes . . . that was it. That was the lesson I needed to learn standing on the dusty streets of Quito. People matter more than projects.

This is a lesson I've failed more times than I want to count. And the problem compounds itself when your identity is tied up in what you do. People can seem like an obstacle to getting what you really want, which is significance.

People matter more than projects.

I remember a time when we had just moved. A new neighborhood and a new school for my children had me feeling very new too. And insecure. And lonely. And wondering, *How will I ever fit in and feel a part of this new community?*

So when my children brought home a flyer for the first PTO (Parent-Teacher Organization) meeting of the school year, I stuck it to the refrigerator, marked the date on the calendar, and decided this was the perfect way to meet other moms like myself. But that wasn't all; I also wanted to use my experience and talents somehow.

The meeting night came, and after a few wrong turns on the unfamiliar campus, I saw a light glowing through the library door. I rushed across the breezeway and walked in with seconds to spare. I'd hoped to meet a few people before the meeting started, but every table was filled with smiling, laughing, we-are-already-friends women. So instead I found a back table and sat next to a father who seemed as out of place as I felt.

Discussion centered around teacher minigrants, playground equipment, trees, and the annual T-shirt sale. The organization was very well run, and at first it seemed they had no need for me. Until the Spring Fun Fest conversation began.

Then it became apparent they needed someone to organize the snack bar. The room was silent when they asked for volunteers. Of course, I should have asked what was involved, but I'd been organizing projects since I led my childhood friends into starting clubs, putting on plays, and hosting backyard fundraising carnivals. So I raised my hand and found myself in charge of running all the food service for the event.

You know that feeling when you are in your sweet spot? That's how I felt organizing the snack bar. This was something I could do easily. I got myself a new pocket folder to keep my notes, added some crisp lined paper, and started making lists. People to call, things to buy, supplies we'd need. *They were going to be amazed at how well this was organized! Maybe it would even be the best snack bar EVER!*

Everything was going great, and then the next PTO meeting arrived. One of the other moms, a veteran PTO gal, walked up to me with a huge smile and said, "I found a great sale on soda, so I picked up some for the snack bar. Let me show you where I stored it."

Rather than appreciating a kind gesture from someone who knew how much work the snack bar really was, I immediately felt defensive. *Did she think I wasn't capable of buying soda for a snack bar?*

I followed her to a storage room and saw stacks of soda—every variety. At that moment, I should have been grateful. I should have oozed thankfulness. But I didn't. She sensed something was wrong but didn't quite know what, and the moment got very awkward.

My insecurities came from a deep desire to prove myself worthy. To show I have what it takes. When my abilities were questioned (at least in my eyes), I felt like a porcupine with its quills standing at attention. And my potential new friend felt the sting of the barbs.

Rather than walking into that situation looking for ways to love my potential new friends, I walked in with pride. Rather than asking for advice and help, I tried to prove something by doing it alone. My approach hindered what my heart really wanted to do: make friends.

How everything changes when my goal in a new situation is to show love to others. Loving others takes the focus off me and my needs. It positions me to serve with humility. It builds up others rather than building up myself.

Just like seeking God before goals, this is an area that needs constant readjusting in my life. I'm always fighting my instincts to get down to business. But every once in a while I get it right.

Just the other day I had a conference call meeting with two coworkers in another city. In the past, the old me would have jumped in to the meeting. That day, I could hear a scratchiness in one of their voices, so I started by asking how she was feeling. The other person was a new employee, although she'd served as an intern, so I knew her. I wanted to let her know how happy I was that she was on our team. After a few moments of chatting, we started the meeting.

The next day I got an email from the first employee, thanking me for asking about her health and welcoming the other employee. My friend knows me, knows how I'm wired, and she noticed and appreciated that I put them first.

People want to know they matter . . . to you and to God. I want to know I matter. And I want to be a woman who takes the time to show love to others before jumping into a project.

Nine

The Sabbath Reset

Years ago I had a small pain on the bottom of my right foot. It was minor, but it was there. Over time it became more painful, causing me to walk with a limp. Finally I could take it no longer and made an appointment with a podiatrist.

The doctor quickly diagnosed me with a plantar wart. Normally those types of growths can be frozen, clipped, or burned off. But because of the location and depth of this one, none of those options would work. This wart would take an incision to remove, but because it was on the pad of my foot, the doctor said the scar would be just as painful.

The only solution was a slow removal by applying a professional-grade chemical wart remover again and again. Which took months. So in that time, I took the maximum amount of painkiller just so I could get around, and I walked with a limp.

Finally the wart went away, as did the pain. But I still limped.

I limped for at least a month after the pain was gone. And each time I'd catch myself limping, I'd have to force myself to walk normally. I conditioned my mind to trust there was no pain, and eventually I was able to walk limp-free.

That experience taught me the power of the mind to keep you in bondage long after you've been set free. Although my experience was physical, I've also experienced feeling in bondage to a behavior that is hard to let go once I've been set free.

This is the power of habit. Whether it's a behavior or thought process, our minds are designed to create neural pathways for anything we repeat consistently. It's like a short-cut that allows our minds to shift into a form of autopilot. Which is why sometimes you panic after leaving the house, wondering if you remembered to lock a door or turn off your curling iron.

Good habits are a blessing. And if you have any, keep them. But bad habits? As anyone who's ever tried knows, they are a beast to change.

This is why overwork is such a powerful habit to break. When you are conditioned to be busy all the time, it will feel uncomfortable to stop. It will feel unnatural, and you will want to retreat back into the comfort of what you know.

For so many years I felt powerless to do anything about the amount of work I had to do. In some ways, I felt like a slave to my to-do list. As you already know about me, I have a track record of overcommitment, and in some bizarre way, I felt like a victim—even though I was a victim of my own making.

What I know now is I'm not a slave to my schedule. I'm not called to be obedient to the requests of others. I *am* called to love and honor those whom God has placed in my life, and I'm to put others before myself, but this is all done in the context of the Lord being the leader of my life.

He's the one I serve and who has assigned me the task of stewarding His call on my life. Whether we are single or married, with or without children, we all answer to God first.

And He wants us to walk in freedom from bondage to any behavior or thought process that hinders us from that obedience.

Changing our allegiance to God means dealing with old habits that chain us to our previous master.

We all serve someone or something. Changing our allegiance to God means dealing with old habits that chain us to our previous master.

That was one of the very first lessons God needed to teach His people, the Israelites, when He called them to Himself. And to help them put God first in all areas of their lives, God established guidelines for living. We call them the Ten Commandments or the law, and one of them specifically speaks to how we manage our time.

As we look to find healthy guidelines for ourselves, it's good to look back and examine what was happening to the Israelites when God gave them the law.

Lest this seem archaic and irrelevant, it would also be good for us to realize that God's principles for living haven't changed. And though we might like to justify doing things our own way, we can learn from past believers that choosing our path never leads to lasting peace or joy.

The Setting for the Ten Commandments

So let's rewind the clock, back to one of the most famous stories in history. It's been recorded on scrolls, passed down through campfire stories, and memorialized on the big screen. It's the story of one of God's most famous acts—the giving of the Ten Commandments.

But before God wrote down ten rules for His people to follow, He set them free from cruel oppression. The Israelites had been enslaved by the Egyptians for four hundred years (Gen. 15:13; Acts 7:6).

It's important for us to understand what it would have been like for the Israelites. The Bible tells us the Egyptians feared the potential power of the Israelite slaves and made a plan to subjugate them. We get a hint of their lives in Exodus 1:11–14:

> So they put slave masters over them to oppress them with forced labor, and they built Pithom and Rameses as store cities for Pharaoh. But the more they were oppressed, the more they multiplied and spread; so the Egyptians came to dread the Israelites and worked them ruthlessly. They made their lives bitter with harsh labor in brick and mortar and with all kinds of work in the fields; in all their harsh labor the Egyptians worked them ruthlessly.

God's people suffered physical, mental, and emotional abuse, and not just for a few years. This slavery went on for generations. Imagine your parents, your grandparents, your great-grandparents, and so on for a few more generations, all living under that kind of oppression.

No ability to choose your own path in life, to develop your own personality or explore your natural gifting. You would have no memory of a day when you got to relax by a river or play with your children. The freedom of individual choice would be a foreign idea.

Your days would consist of doing what other people told you to do. Seven days a week. This kind of life changes the way you think, and God knew that.

God had a plan to set His children free. Not just from physical slavery, but from mental slavery.

First, God had to free them physically, so He sent Moses to demand their freedom from Pharaoh. Pharaoh wasn't agreeable, so God sent a series of ten plagues to "convince" Pharaoh that letting the Israelites go was the right thing to do. Finally, after the tenth and most devastating plague when every firstborn son in Egypt died, Pharaoh released the Israelites.

If you've read Exodus, you know there's more to this powerful story, including the very first Passover, which was a foreshadow of the coming of Jesus. That night of the tenth plague, the Israelites were instructed to put the blood of a blemish-free lamb over and on the sides of their doors. In those homes the firstborn was saved.

Today, through the blood of Jesus, the sinless lamb, we are saved from our sins. It's a story worth studying in greater detail, but for now we are going to move on in the story—past two million Israelites packing up and leaving Egypt, past the parting of the Red Sea, past the Israelites crossing on dry land, and past the Egyptian army being swallowed up when the water was reunited.

God had miraculously rescued His people and now planned to take them to the Promised Land, a land set apart for those who would call on the name of Yahweh. But as we know from Scripture, it wasn't a direct, easy, or quick journey.

The Lord had His purposes for this time in the desert, and everything that happened was intentionally to train, teach, and test the Israelites.

God's desire was a relationship. He was calling this people His own, and they would call Him their God. We see His intentions back in Exodus 6:2–7:

> God also said to Moses, "I am the LORD. I appeared to Abraham, to Isaac and to Jacob as God Almighty, but by my name the LORD I did not make myself fully known to them. I also established my covenant with them to give them the land of Canaan, where they resided as foreigners. Moreover, I have heard the groaning of the Israelites, whom the Egyptians are enslaving, and I have remembered my covenant.
>
> "Therefore, say to the Israelites: 'I am the LORD, and I will bring you out from under the yoke of the Egyptians. I will free you from being slaves to them, and I will redeem you with an outstretched arm and with mighty acts of judgment. I will take you as my own people, and I will be your God. Then you will know that I am the LORD your God, who brought you out from under the yoke of the Egyptians.'"

God rescued His people from slavery to keep His promise and to show them His love and faithfulness. Plus, He wanted them to know His power to act in and through them if they would only trust Him. But learning to trust God was difficult for these people with a slave mindset.

For so many years growing up, and then as a new Christian, I learned this story and marveled at God's power. I knew the story of the Exodus and how ungrateful the Israelites were.

And I read the Ten Commandments and thought about them as good rules for us as we serve God and live together on this earth. But it wasn't until a few years ago that I realized the Ten Commandments were a transition plan.

They were God's plan to transition His people from living as *slaves* of an earthly king to *children* of a heavenly King. God's people had to shift their allegiance, and in order to do so, they had to trust God.

The Bible tells us the Israelites were overjoyed when they were set free, but very quickly they grumbled about the harsh conditions. God was compassionate and provided for their needs. They were thirsty, and God provided water. They were hungry, and God rained down bread they called manna. When they got tired of manna, God sent quail.

But God didn't just want to give them food. Satisfying physical hunger wouldn't create the trusting relationship God desired. God wanted to heal their hearts and minds from generations of bondage, and that would only come through dependence on One who was completely trustworthy.

The Israelites needed to trust God would protect rather than abandon, and redeem rather than exploit.

Trust wasn't easy then, and it isn't easy now.

In the midst of meeting their physical needs, God made a request that would start to meet their heart needs. Before God ever gave them the Ten Commandments, the very first trust-training exercise had to do with *not* working one day a week.

God told Moses He would send down "bread from heaven," but the people were to only gather enough for that day. No more. And on the sixth day they were to gather twice as much. This was because on the seventh day they were to take a "Sabbath rest" and there would be no bread from heaven (Exod. 16:23).

Of course, the people didn't trust God at first and tried to save some of the manna overnight. Only in the morning it was filled with maggots. When hoarding an extra supply didn't work, they tried gathering manna on the seventh day, but there was none.

It's not that God didn't want them to have enough to eat. He did, and they had enough. But He wanted them to retrain their brains to look to Him as their provider. This trust would break the slave mindset that pervaded the Israelites' minds.

It seems like such a simple thing, really. Yet why was it so hard? God had shown the Israelites His power in miracle after miracle. They'd seen things with their own eyes that we only read about. He'd freed them, protected them, led them, and fed them with His mighty hand. And all He asked was that they not gather food on the Sabbath and trust Him to care for them.

But they didn't.

Oh, how I understand the power of the mind to keep someone in bondage. While I have never experienced slavery or even deprivation, in 2005 my husband and I adopted two little girls from Liberia, Africa, who had experienced both.

At that time, Liberia was just coming out of a brutal civil war, where the people literally destroyed their country. Actually, the country had gone through two civil wars, the first from 1989 to 1996 and the second from 1999 to 2003. So it was a double whammy. In 2005 they were just beginning to put their country back together, but it was still a war zone.

Our daughters were born in 1995 and 1998, and they experienced atrocities and deprivation no child ever should.

Their early lives consisted of neglect, insufficient food, dirty water, no education, no health care, and exploitation at the hands of adults they should have been able to trust.

Their physical health was relatively easy to repair. It didn't take long before their little bodies were strong and healthy. But their emotional and mental wounds were deep, and trust was at the root of every challenge we faced, especially with our younger daughter.

Deep in her brain, she didn't trust adults. This lack of trust manifested in daily decisions to do things her way. Subconsciously she believed no one could be trusted. Especially not a new mother when, in her mind, her biological mother didn't protect her.

So many times I asked her to trust me. She'd only seen goodness at my hand, she'd only been loved and cared for with tenderness. I'd never abandoned her or neglected her. And yet she didn't trust me. Countless times a day, in small and big ways, she did the opposite of what I asked.

Our story is still being written, so I'm careful with what I share. But after years of spiritual and professional help, that trust was still not there. My daughter did not, and does not, trust me. Her resistance to trust and obedience has caused all of us much pain.

This is why I don't judge the Israelites, nor do I judge anyone who has been through abuse. It's really hard to trust when your trust has been betrayed. To trust again takes a depth of bravery few have.

However, it is worth the risk when we look to God, because He alone is utterly trustworthy.

Through the pain of someone not trusting me, I learned a life-changing truth: the depth of our relationships is equivalent to the degree we trust the other person. This is true with every person in our lives, and it's definitely true with God. We can only go as deep as we trust.

If I don't trust you, I will withhold parts of myself. I will guard my heart, only sharing what feels safe. I will carefully construct a façade and even then will keep you at a distance.

We can only go as deep as we trust.

My relationship with God was distant for years because of my shallow trust. I loved Him and served Him with all my heart. But trust Him? Not really, and my life was proof.

There was too much fear, too much control, and too much pride in everything I did. My fear caused anxiety, my control caused overwork, and my pride created a moral superiority that did not please God, thus causing more distance.

I knew God could answer any prayer, but deep in my heart I didn't think He'd answer mine.

My lack of faith brought me to a crossroads when my fear of flying caused me to stop flying, and even caused me to avoid driving by the airport. God did a miracle in my heart because now I fly fear-free—even with lots of turbulence and bumpy landings. But part of my healing was uncovering misplaced trust.

Rather than trusting God to protect me, I was trusting the pilot . . . or the weather . . . or the air traffic controller . . . or the mechanic to have done his job in the engine precheck. But I knew I couldn't completely trust any of that, hence my fear.

Part of my victory over fear was identifying, one by one, everything I trusted rather than God. It took some digging, because fear is sneaky. It confuses your mind and causes you to react in self-protective ways. But I was so tired of being afraid, that I prayed and God started to show me what I was trusting.

Then I took every doubting thought captive and intentionally chose to trust God. I would even say it out loud: "I don't trust the weather, I trust *You*."

If anyone wants proof that God is real, I'm a walking testimony. Every time I've dealt with fear, I apply this same exercise: I identify what I'm trusting to keep me or my loved ones safe, and I call it out. Each time I've intentionally chosen to trust God rather than whatever else I had been trusting.

God continues to take me on this journey of faith by asking me, "Do you trust Me or do you just say that you trust Me?"

Years ago my honest answer was, "I just say I trust You." But with each identification of misplaced trust, and each reassignment to the only One who is truly trustworthy, my relationship with God has gone places I never imagined. It's hard to remember the fear that laced so much of who I was.

But let's go back to the Israelites. This is the depth of faith God was trying to instill in the Israelites. Yet we can sense their fear and confusion. A slave mentality is always one of fear. And fear motivations are always self-protecting.

But God knew He could be trusted, and so the very first act of faith God asked from His people had to do with not working on the Sabbath. That's it. Rather than working seven days a week, God told the people to only work six.

What a beautiful, loving way for God to try to teach living by faith—ask people who have worked nonstop to rest.

And yet their bondage to work went deeper than the physical. They probably struggled, just like we do, with thinking they had to work in order to meet their needs.

God's lessons of faith didn't stop there. The Israelites continued on their journey to the Promised Land, and after three months they came to the desert of Sinai. And this is where God got very intentional about giving His people guidelines for a relationship with Him and with each other. It was on the mountain where the Lord called Moses and gave him the Ten Commandments.

The fact that the Israelites had been in slavery was integral to the giving of the Ten Commandments, and God confirms that with the introduction, "I am the LORD your God, who brought you out of Egypt, out of the land of slavery" (Exod. 20:2).

God proceeded to give Moses the foundation for becoming a people who are not enslaved, who serve a loving God. The first commandment was to have no other gods before the Lord. The second was to not make images for the people to worship (which, ironically, the people happened to be doing at that very moment). The third was to not misuse the name of the Lord. And the fourth was to remember the Sabbath and keep it holy.

What the Lord introduced in the desert with collecting manna on six days only, He confirmed on a tablet written with His finger.

The Sabbath Reset

Taking a day of rest was critical to breaking the slave mindset because it reset their focus once a week. We see this command again in Deuteronomy 5, which is where the Ten Commandments are repeated. In this passage, God presents the Sabbath commandment this way:

Remember that you were slaves in Egypt and that the LORD your God brought you out of there with a mighty hand and an outstretched arm. Therefore the LORD your God has commanded you to observe the Sabbath day. (Deut. 5:15)

Observing the Sabbath is the only command linked to slavery, which is why it has practical application for us today.

We who have felt helpless to overwork, we who have felt victimized by the demands of others, we who have been enslaved to our schedules . . . we need our minds transformed from a slave mindset to a free mindset. The Sabbath was meant for us.

No other practice has reset my mind and heart like observing the Sabbath. But it did not come easy.

For years I tried to find the loophole. For example, I found a passage in Leviticus describing the festivals, and I read a verse about the closing assembly where the Israelites were told to do "no regular work" (Lev. 23:36). So I excused my working on the Sabbath because it wasn't work that had to do with my employment. But it was still work.

God was chipping away at all the areas of my life where I displayed a lack of trust, and observing the Sabbath was one of my final strongholds.

When I uncovered my doubt, like I did with my fear of flying, the truth was evident: I didn't trust the Lord to help me get all my work done in six days. Once again, I thought it all depended on me.

The more I've deliberately chosen to rest on the Sabbath, the more my enslavement to overwork has lessened. No amount of my trying to shake off those chains made a difference. But as I've declared my trust in God through honoring the Sabbath, the chains have fallen off.

God created a need for Sabbath rest deep within us. Jesus even said, "The Sabbath was made for man, not man for the Sabbath" (Mark 2:27). Just like a loving parent puts a toddler down for a nap and sets healthy bedtimes, so God puts parameters around our week to get us to stop working because we need it.

God created a need for Sabbath rest deep within us.

There is one more profound purpose of the Sabbath. It was a sign of the promise made between God and His people. In Exodus 31:13, God spoke to Moses: "Say to the Israelites, 'You must observe my Sabbaths. This will be a sign between me and you for the generations to come, so you may know that I am the LORD, who makes you holy.'"

God wants us to physically rest from our work, and in doing so, we mark ourselves as followers of God. It's like once a week we redeclare who we follow.

Of all the commandments, I find this one easiest to break because there's not a direct link to the consequences. And yet my overwhelmed life and track record of regrets are compelling proof there are indeed consequences.

What a beautiful gift our Father gives us in the Sabbath. An opportunity to rest. A chance to trust. A mental reset from slave to free. And an invitation to experience His faithfulness, all while we enjoy ourselves. The Sabbath is a gift I want to open every week.

Ten

Is It Ever Okay to Quit?

We often want to quit when things get hard. Whether it's learning something new, joining a group where we are the outsider, or being around people who don't treat us like we deserve to be treated, most of us find ourselves in a difficult situation at some time or other, and getting out seems like the best avenue.

But achievement-oriented people don't believe in quitting. We know that sometimes trial by fire is the only path to success. And we can't guarantee that in every life situation everything will go smoothly.

Not only does our internal wiring push us past our limits at times, but the Bible holds a promise for persevering. Romans 5:3–4 is clear there's an internal benefit when we don't give up in the face of suffering: "Not only so, but we also glory in our sufferings, because we know that suffering produces perseverance; perseverance, character; and character, hope."

But sometimes I've wondered if it's ever okay to quit. I've wrestled with this question for decades. I've faced situation after situation where I've asked if there's a right and wrong decision. I've sought biblical answers and asked the Lord for wisdom.

Sometimes we need to give ourselves the grace and permission to quit that which we've committed to.

And after all that seeking, I'm convinced that sometimes it's okay to quit. Sometimes, even though our decision seemed right at the beginning, situations change and what we thought would happen didn't. People change. We change. Truth is uncovered, weakness discovered.

We don't have the ability to see the future, and even our best decisions are still limited by human abilities and insight. Sometimes we need to give ourselves the grace and permission to quit that which we've committed to.

David Allen, author of *Getting Things Done*, calls this renegotiating the contract with ourselves. We must learn to re-evaluate and adjust expectations based on new circumstances. We do this in business all the time when increased costs or unforeseen challenges arise. So why is it so hard to admit that we need course corrections in our own lives?

When our significance is connected with work, stepping back is a scary concept. Quitting feels like failure . . . meaning we'd *be* a failure. But in this chapter, I'd like to dig a bit deeper and identify some situations where quitting is the right thing to do.

As women who tend toward living with overloaded lives, there will be times when we need to remove a responsibility, resign a position, or abandon a goal.

To start, let's see what Scripture has to say about it. Throughout the Bible we are encouraged to press on, persevere, not give up hope, be brave, believe, and trust the Lord to strengthen us as we face our challenges. Is there anywhere we are encouraged to stop?

The answer is yes, and we find a powerful reason to quit given by Jesus Himself.

When It Causes You to Sin

In the middle of the Sermon on the Mount, Jesus speaks about adultery. And while He's certainly teaching about the dangers of adultery, He's also teaching about the principle of sin. Sin isn't just the *act* of disobedience; it's what happens before that, in our hearts. This teaching was radical to the Jews, who believed they were doing fine when they obeyed their list of 613 rules and regulations, called the *mitzvot*.

Jesus taught that sin in our hearts is just as bad as the sin we commit with our words or actions. Regarding adultery, Jesus said that whoever even *looks* at a woman with lust has committed adultery (Matt. 5:28). I imagine there were some dropped eyes and shuffling of feet at *that* proclamation.

Then Jesus describes the drastic attitude we should have about our sin in verses 29–30:

> If your right eye causes you to stumble, gouge it out and throw it away. It is better for you to lose one part of your body than for your whole body to be thrown into hell. And if your right hand causes you to stumble, cut it off and throw it away. It is better for you to lose one part of your body than for your whole body to go into hell.

We understand Jesus is using exaggeration to make His point, since even a blind person can sin in their heart. The message is we are to choose a swift and dramatic response to whatever causes us to sin.

Sometimes this can be done in a mental 180-degree turn while we stay in the same place. Sometimes when we become aware of a sin, we can confess it and God brings immediate change into our hearts and actions.

Other times the situation is too difficult to stay in, or we aren't mature enough to handle it. In those instances, we need to quit.

This happened to me when I'd been asked to serve as the children's ministry director at my small church. It was a great part-time job that seemed manageable. I had three small children at the time, so I was already involved in that ministry. And because I have the gift of teaching and administration, it seemed a perfect fit.

For a while everything went great. I loved helping pick out curriculum and organizing the teacher supply room. I liked working with the other leaders, who shared a similar passion for teaching. And I loved the children.

Where this job fell apart for me was with the volunteers. Every week it seemed somebody called to cancel, or worse yet, just didn't show up. And most often I deemed their excuses flimsy at best. After all, *I* didn't let a headache stop me from showing up. And *I* went to bed early on Saturday night so I wasn't too tired to show up.

Week after week I grew more and more annoyed. Especially since I was often the one to fill in for that volunteer, meaning I missed the church service I desperately needed.

I grew prideful as I compared my commitment with others

and found them lacking. I grew resentful at their lack of dedication, and my compassion meter ran on empty.

After a year of praying and asking for God's strength and trying to resolve these issues through practical means, my heart was steadfastly in the wrong place. I didn't like the person I was becoming, and I went to the pastor and gave notice (and stayed till we found a replacement).

There are a few reasons I couldn't handle that job. First, my energy and compassion were pretty much consumed by raising three little boys. Second, pride had a firm hold of me back then, and I was starting to see that it would take much to root it out. And third, I just wasn't spiritually mature enough to handle the job.

Being on staff at a church requires a depth of spiritual and emotional maturity I didn't have. I didn't have the undergirding of personal prayer nor did I know how to handle all the knowledge that came with that position. It was absolutely the right decision to quit; I've never second-guessed that one.

As you consider all your commitments and responsibilities, is there one where you know either your thoughts, words, or actions aren't right? If so, it's always best to seek God's help before quitting.

God might have you in this situation to develop your character. So dig in to your prayer life and study God's Word. God has used hard situations to convict and correct me of sin. There have been plenty of other times I wanted to quit a responsibility due to my own sin, but God kept me there and changed me.

But if you are in a situation where you are continually tempted to sin, or are already in sin, and you don't feel equipped to handle it, you could be facing the go-ahead to quit.

When We Cause Others to Stumble

Jesus spoke of another instance where we are to deal dramatically with our situation, and that is when we cause others to stumble.

Sometimes we are in a place of influence and use that influence inappropriately. I believe Jesus's first choice in any situation is that we change immediately and experience His power and victory over sin. And yet we read again in Matthew 18 that Jesus champions doing whatever it takes to eliminate the cause of sin.

Jesus had just taught the disciples the importance of humility in the kingdom of heaven, of becoming childlike in our hearts and welcoming children in His name. Then Jesus continued with another scathing warning to those who cause others to stumble when they follow Him:

> Woe to the world because of the things that cause people to stumble! Such things must come, but woe to the person through whom they come! If your hand or your foot causes you to stumble, cut it off and throw it away. It is better for you to enter life maimed or crippled than to have two hands or two feet and be thrown into eternal fire. And if your eye causes you to stumble, gouge it out and throw it away. It is better for you to enter life with one eye than to have two eyes and be thrown into the fire of hell. (Matt. 18:7–9)

For most of us, this reason to quit is harder to identify. It's easy to point the finger at others or at circumstances as the cause of our sin. That comes super easy for me. But to honestly assess myself as the problem or as a contributor to the problem? Uh . . . not so easy.

As I've thought of ways to apply this to our discussion, it would seem these circumstances don't always have to involve sin. Sin is obvious. For example, if I'm taking office supplies home from my job and telling others it's okay to take home staplers and reams of paper, then it's pretty clear I'm leading others to sin.

But sometimes the problem could just be a clash of personalities or a different approach to a challenge. I've been in collaborative situations where it becomes obvious I have a different style of work than my partners. If my approach is causing frustration or dissension to others, then it might be a sign to quit my involvement.

That's not always possible in work situations. Employers are seldom worried about the spiritual danger of conflict. But in other environments, it might be more important to keep the peace and friendships than to force our way. Even though there's no sin involved, it's a humble choice to acknowledge we might be a stumbling block for others.

Sometimes we need to be alert to the potential hidden within others and step down so they can step up.

Romans 12:18 says, "If it is possible, as far as it depends on you, live at peace with everyone." Sometimes it might depend on us stepping away from a commitment.

There's another side to this idea, and it's that sometimes we need to quit not because we cause people to stumble in sin but because we hinder their growth.

We've probably all seen the woman who takes on all the responsibilities, then complains because she's doing all the work. She loves the glory and the martyrdom at the same time. The truth is there are others who could help, who could step up and use their gifts and talents, but there's no opportunity because of Miss Superstar.

Sometimes we need to be alert to the potential hidden within others and step down so they can step up. This is part of living an others-centered life and is truly for the best of the kingdom as well.

When Your Inner Resources Are Insufficient

Sometimes despite our best efforts our inner self isn't strong enough to handle the work or the pressure. This is what happened to my son Robbie one year playing football.

He stuck with that football team the entire season. He was at every game and every practice and gave it his all. Only his little heart never adjusted to the style of coaching that year, which was more negative than positive. This was evidenced by his stomachaches stopping immediately after that season was over.

Even though he was raised in the same home as his two older brothers, at that stage of his life he didn't have the confidence they had. His oldest brother, Josh, had suffered through a bad season of coaching a few years earlier and was able to brush it off. The criticism didn't affect him the way it affected Robbie.

We all walk into situations with weaknesses and vulnerabilities based on our past or current circumstances. We all react differently to the hardships of life. What one person can handle with ease brings another to her knees.

The most unfair thing we can do to ourselves is compare our capabilities to someone else's (or even to ourselves from another time in our lives) and think, "Surely I can do this thing if I just try hard enough." Sometimes we can try all we want, but we don't have the inner resources to support our outer commitments.

Earlier in the chapter I referenced a time when I stepped down from my position as children's ministry director due in part to the high level of demand from my three small children. That wasn't the only time my inner resources weren't sufficient.

Years later when we adopted our daughters, I went through another demanding and emotionally draining time, which I also mentioned earlier. At that time, I stopped public speaking after the girls joined our family.

A few years later I tried to pick back up and speak again, but I couldn't do it. I didn't have the mental energy to prepare, I didn't have the physical energy to add that to my part-time job, and I honestly didn't have the spiritual strength to teach others when I was struggling so much at home.

The problem was I had a book contract, and publishers expect you to speak. So when I stepped down from the speaker team at Proverbs 31 Ministries, I fully thought I was giving up my writing career as well. But I didn't have it in me to travel and speak. Even though I loved to teach women in a group setting, I had to quit.

After making that decision, the Lord did the sweetest thing. It didn't happen immediately, but very soon He brought me opportunities to teach from home through our COMPEL online writer training program.

The Lord knew my heart was to teach, but it wasn't wise or healthy for me to continue on in the way I was doing it. Quitting public speaking opened the door for the Lord to do something new in my life.

If I had insisted on speaking even though it caused immense stress on me and my family, I would have missed out on the blessing the Lord had planned.

When You Really Aren't Good at Something

The final good reason to quit is when you aren't doing what you were made to do. Now, most of us were raised in a culture where we were told we could do anything we set our minds to. There was no limit to where we could go or what we could do. We have this thought ingrained in us that to access our potential we have to identify, classify, and rectify our weaknesses.

Want to be a doctor? Sure you can! Despite the fact that you can't stand the sight of blood.

How about an engineer? Of course! Only you might need to be good at math or chemistry or physics.

But what happens when it's just not possible to fix your weaknesses?

I knew early on my skill set didn't include athletics, but I was pretty confident of my academic prowess. While others loved to play kickball and volleyball at recess, I was happier volunteering in the library or working on a project.

I excelled at most every class. I was a straight-A student in anything with words, including English and Spanish. History had lots of words, and I was great at outlining chapters and memorizing facts, so I sailed through those classes. With a little effort and lots of practice, I could understand most basic math and science concepts.

However, my supersized opinion of my intellectual abilities took its first hit when I enrolled in chemistry in college. It was like I ran straight into a brick wall.

It wasn't that I didn't try. I joined study groups, sought private tutoring, worked with my lab partner as often as I could, and still sat at the kitchen table every night crying because I couldn't understand it.

I just couldn't seem to visualize what I couldn't see. *How can you remember how many neutrons and protons are in carbon when you can't see subatomic particles?*

I'm pretty sure I failed every test. For an honor student to even get a C is like a living nightmare . . . and this was like the zombie apocalypse.

There was only one way I passed that class, and it was lab. My partner just happened to be a college chemistry professor's daughter! Imagine that! And when you took my F in the class portion of the grade and added it to the A in lab, I actually passed chemistry. Let's just say it wasn't pretty.

Sometimes we just aren't good at things. We don't have the natural aptitude or spiritual gifting or intellectual ability to manage certain things. I learned I'm an extremely concrete thinker. This makes me very good at editing and organizing things I can touch. Conversely, I'm very weak at visualizing a master plan or seeing how big numbers fit together. And obviously I couldn't solve a chemistry problem if my life depended on it.

There are things I just don't do well. No matter how much I want to excel, I can't.

I face that today in my work situation when we start talking about budgets and forecasts and ROI. I want to be the manager who understands all that lingo, but whatever kept me from understanding chemistry hinders me from excelling at certain business tasks.

And today I'm okay with that. What a blessing to be able to write those words.

God didn't create me by accident. He did so with great intentionality and love, and made every fiber of my body and every cell in my brain to be exactly the way He wanted it. Even my weaknesses are no mistake or surprise to Him.

He created me to do the work He planned for me. And He did the same for you.

For four long, painful months in that chemistry class, I felt stupid. Seriously. I questioned my ability to do any kind of academics. I remember thinking maybe I needed to give up college since I was going to have to take another science class. (Side note to all college and university staff: please reconsider making English or journalism students take chemistry—thank you.)

But that wasn't at all true. Chemistry's just not my talent. I have plenty of other ones, just not that.

We've all got these areas in our lives. For some of you, numbers make your heart sing and words make you want to cry. I get that . . . only in the opposite way.

When we find ourselves in jobs or responsibilities that don't fit how we are made, we might need to consider quitting. When we keep trying and trying to fix what we think is broken, we waste so much energy and can do so much damage.

I love how authors Marcus Buckingham and Curt Coffman put it in their book *First, Break All the Rules*:

> Persistence directed primarily toward your nontalents is self-destructive—no amount of determination or good intentions will ever enable you to carve out a brand-new set of four-lane mental highways. You will reprimand yourself, berate yourself and put yourself through all manner of contortions in an attempt to achieve the impossible.[9]

I know there are all kinds of exceptions to the idea of quitting when we aren't naturally gifted in an area. Sometimes we do need to learn something or get stronger in certain areas and then stay where we are. Sometimes we fill in where we are needed in an emergency, and it would be an extreme hardship on someone else if we quit just because it wasn't a sweet spot. But I'm talking about long-term commitments where it's clear we weren't designed to be.

Being in the wrong place using the wrong skills keeps us from being in the right place using the right skills.

Here's what I've learned: it's never too late to change direction.

I've also learned that every lesson in life has a cost. You might be reading this and feel you are too far into something to quit now based on how much money, time, or energy you've spent. You aren't. That's just how much it cost you to learn this lesson. So stop now and redirect.

Being in the wrong place using the wrong skills keeps us from being in the right place using the right skills. And wrong place/wrong skill assignments are draining. But right place/right skill assignments are life-giving.

I know the idea of quitting anything can feel wrong. But when we do it in the right way, for the right reasons, it can be one of the best ways to get ourselves on a healthy track of life.

Eleven

How to Find Sustainable Balance

My husband's grandfather was a pastor, and we were blessed to have him perform our marriage ceremony. Like most giddy brides, I don't remember much of what he said, except one statement: "Don't expect marriage to always be fifty-fifty. One of you will always be giving more than the other."

This was lived out starting day one of our marriage. From there on out, it was never a fifty-fifty arrangement. Some days I felt like I was giving 60 percent to the marriage while my husband was only putting forth 40 percent. Then there were other days when he was making more effort than I was. However, the math always made sense because we ended up with 100 percent.

This philosophy of equality is one we carry with us everywhere. Whether we are talking about effort, a cake, or a dollar bill, we have a whole at some point, then fractions of that whole.

The problem comes when we try to apply this concept of balance to our lives. We desperately want balance, but we believe that will happen when we divide up the responsibilities and priorities with the amount of time we have.

For example, we all have 168 hours in a week. Approximately 49 of those are taken up with sleep, while another 40 are assigned to work. Then there's commute time at another 5 hours a week. What's left is 74 hours. In those hours we need to care for our homes, grocery shop, help with homework, go to church, and so much more.

For overbusy women, there's always a quiet sense of despair there isn't enough of us to go around.

If we lived in a pie chart, it might actually make sense. Because if we kept a diary of every minute spent in a week, we *would* get to 100 percent. On paper, we could make our lives fit into the diagram.

So if finding balance is as easy as a math problem, then why do so many of us get to the end of the week feeling out of sync and with a list of regrets? We wish we had spent more time on some things and less time on others. And the list of things we didn't get done is often longer than the completed list. For overbusy women, there's always a quiet sense of despair there isn't enough of us to go around.

Not enough mom for our children.
Not enough wife for our husband.
Not enough friend . . . not enough daughter . . . not enough volunteer . . . not enough employee.

The needs always seem to be greater than we have capacity to meet, and we worry someone is always disappointed.

And herein lies the problem. We don't live in a pie chart. It's much more of a bar graph—you know, the kind where the bars can dip under the baseline. That's us. There are times we get so busy we run a deficit.

Our lives are run more by the concept of how our inner resources meet our external demands. Every responsibility we have demands something from us. Some demands we meet with ease. These are the tasks and assignments we feel we were made for. They renew us and give us joy.

This is how I felt for years singing backup on the praise team at church. I looked forward to practice and loved Sundays. If I got to be on the team that sang at Easter, it truly felt like I was playing in the Super Bowl.

Then there are other tasks and responsibilities that feel like they drain the life out of you. You might love these responsibilities, but they aren't easy. Often this is how moms of young children feel, especially when their children's temperament isn't docile. Maybe you have that kid you are sure is going to be president one day! You'd never complain, but when your wee one finally goes to sleep, you collapse.

Our lives are run more by the concept of how our inner resources meet our external demands.

Our lives are made up of all kinds of demands, from the ones that make our hearts sing to the ones that bring us to tears. Each one requires something different from us. If we plow ahead trying to find balance and divide up a pie chart of time, only looking at the time a responsibility takes, we will never find it.

Is Balance Really Important?

The Bible doesn't say anything about living a balanced life. So why is it important?

It's true the Bible doesn't talk about balance, but it says a lot about obedience. We obey God in two ways: in our hearts and in our deeds. In the Old Testament book of 1 Samuel we read about King Saul facing God's anger over his disobedience. God gave Saul very clear and drastic instructions to completely destroy an enemy nation, including all the livestock. Saul partially obeyed but decided in his own heart to bring back the best sheep and cattle for a sacrifice.

Through the prophet Samuel, God spoke these words to Saul: "Does the Lord delight in burnt offerings and sacrifices as much as in obeying the Lord? To obey is better than sacrifice, and to heed is better than the fat of rams" (1 Sam. 15:22).

So while God only asks us to listen and obey (which can be a sacrifice!), sometimes we decide we know what's best. We'd rather decide what to sacrifice. We run ourselves into the ground thinking we are serving the Lord, sacrificing our health, our families, the quality of our work, and our sanity. And according to 1 Samuel 15, the Lord does not delight in it.

To prepare our lives for acts of obedience, we must live with a healthy balance.

The Process of Finding Balance

Finding balance begins with identifying and accepting our internal resources. This process can actually be fun, as most of us enjoy discovering the unique ways God made us. Our design was *not* haphazard. The Bible tells us God designed us with a purpose in mind.

Ephesians 2:10 says, "For we are God's handiwork, created in Christ Jesus to do good works, which God prepared in advance for us to do." And to the prophet Jeremiah God said, "Before I made you in your mother's womb, I chose you. Before you were born, I set you apart for a special work" (Jer. 1:5 NCV).

The more we discover how God made us, complete with our inner strengths and gifts, the more we can make wise choices about what to do with our time and energy.

Finding balance begins with identifying and accepting our internal resources.

You may not feel as if you have any special gifts or talents, but you do. Everyone does. We were shaped by a Master Artist for a purpose.

Pastor and author Rick Warren uses the acronym SHAPE to help us understand our unique design. It's an excellent overview of the different "design elements" of our lives. SHAPE stands for:

Spiritual gifts
Heart
Abilities
Personality
Experience

You can read more about the concept in his excellent book, *The Purpose-Driven Life*. For now, it's enough to know you have a shape—a God-designed one.

We also have other types of resources that impact how much we can manage and still stay balanced.

Internal Resources

Besides our SHAPE, there are other resources we have that impact what it will take for us to manage our responsibilities. First, there are the fruits of the Spirit. These are listed in Galatians 5:22: love, joy, peace, patience, kindness, goodness, faithfulness, gentleness, and self-control. It would be wonderful if we had all these fruits in fullness, but we are works in progress. I used to think I had an overflowing of the fruit of patience, until I had kids. Then somehow it got squashed. It took years for me to learn to submit to the Holy Spirit and stop trying to do things in my flesh before I saw that fruit again.

Spiritual maturity also plays a role in what I can manage. Early in my walk with the Lord, there were things I wasn't ready for. I already mentioned being children's ministry director, but I also spent time serving on a top leadership council in my church when I was in my midtwenties. I had the spiritual gift of leadership but not the maturity I needed to manage at that level. I needed to use my gift of leadership in smaller venues before I grew in spiritual maturity.

Physical Resources

Physically, each of us is wired differently. Some have high levels of energy, others have low. Some need seven hours of sleep, others need nine. Some have chronic health issues, others seem free of health concerns.

Years ago, my dear friend Susanne Scheppmann wrote a devotion I've always remembered. She titled it "Wired Tired."

In it Susanne said, "I have never been a high-energy gal. My energy and stamina ebb on the low side. It seems when God created me, he wired me tired."[10]

That was the first time I remember realizing my wiring was God-inspired. And just as Susanne accepted her "low wattage" energy level, I need to accept mine and not apologize for it.

The Lord wants to use us all, in whatever physical condition we find ourselves. Our physical abilities or disabilities aren't a hindrance to God, and it's okay to consider our physical resources when making choices.

Relational and Financial Resources

Relational resources are the friends and family who support us, especially when times are rough. Establishing a solid group of people we can depend on makes us stronger, healthier, and happier. Also, working outside our financial resources can be crippling. It's wise to not overextend ourselves and to stay financially healthy.

Finding our healthy balance won't look like other people's balance. The worst thing we can do is compare ourselves to others, and heaven help us if we judge. The Lord has created us to manage the responsibilities and priorities He assigns, and they will be different from our neighbor's responsibilities and priorities.

The most important thing is to keep our eyes on our heavenly Father for direction, wisdom, and strength. And when we do that, we will find His healthy balance for our lives.

Twelve

How to Be Peaceful and Productive

"How do you get so much done?"

That's a question I've been asked many times in my life. For years I took pride in my response, because if you only look at surface data, perhaps I do accomplish more than others. Maybe I can plow through more tasks or keep my kitchen organized and counters clean. I can meet deadlines and submit projects that are sufficient.

I've always longed to be a highly productive person. My bookcase filled with time-management books and planners, and my phone filled with time-saving apps and hacks, is proof.

However, I've learned that's a superficial way to look at productivity. I don't want to get more done; I want to get more of the right things done.

Getting things done provides an immediate relief, but getting the right things done brings peace. That's what I want: peaceful productivity.

I don't want to get more done; I want to get more of the right things done. At the end of the day, if my to-do list is filled with check marks but I've neglected what's most important in my life, I will lay my head on the pillow and still feel unrest. There will be an unease of things left undone.

That's productivity without peace. That's not my goal. So how do I go about being busy with the right things?

My journey to a more peaceful, productive place has been filled with steps forward and steps back. But with God's help, I'm making progress. In this chapter, I want to share a few more practices that have made the biggest difference in my life.

Live a God-Directed Life Rather Than a Self-Directed Life

As I hung up the blank calendar in my kitchen each January, empty of appointments but full of promise, I declared to myself, "This year will be different!"

My resolve was firm and I was full of unbridled optimism. I was convinced this would be *the* year.

This would be the year I finally got my schedule under control, finished that house project, got consistent in exercise, lost weight, prayed faithfully, spent more time with friends, and so on and so forth.

And yet, for so many years I'd get to March (if I lasted that long) and give up on my goals, feeling like a failure once again.

I got so frustrated with myself because I knew how to do this stuff. I might not do it perfectly, but I can paint a wall, take a walk, put less food in my mouth, sit and pray, and schedule time with friends. This isn't rocket science! But for some reason I either stopped trying or kept making the same choices as before, expecting a different result.

It's hard to keep pressing on to make positive changes in your life when you feel like you've tried everything and nothing works. It's so easy to give up and accept the status quo, thinking, "I'll never change. This is hopeless."

Hopelessness is one of the worst feelings in the world, second only to fear. And when those two emotions are combined, we will retreat to what seems safe and secure, even though it drives us crazy.

After living an out-of-control busy life for so many years, I was on a first-name basis with hopelessness and fear. The worst part was, I got myself there; I was in the driver's seat to chaos.

Looking back, I don't ever remember asking God for advice on whether or not I should take on a certain responsibility. If I could do it, I said yes. From a human point of view, that should have empowered me. But the truth is, a self-driven life eventually leads to a place of hopelessness because there is an end to *our* power.

I wonder if the disciples felt hopeless the night they went fishing and caught nothing. The story is told in John 21, after Jesus's death and resurrection, when the disciples had gone to Galilee to wait for Him (see Matt. 26:32).

While in Galilee, at least on one night, the disciples returned to their old lives . . . to fishing. They knew how to fish, they'd done it all their lives, they were born to fish. But that night, after hours sitting in wooden boats and floating in the silent dark, they caught nothing.

Let's pause there a moment and consider how they must have felt. They must have been confused, with unanswered questions about their past and future. Had the last three years been a waste of time? What were they supposed to do next? And now they failed at something they knew how to do.

For all of us who feel like failures because we can't get things done, it's good to know even the disciples understood that feeling.

The story takes an interesting turn as the sun starts to rise. On the edge of the lake stood Jesus (although they didn't recognize Him at first). I'm sure He'd been watching them for hours . . . maybe even all night. And I suspect He told the fish to stay back from the boat for a while. After all, He directed the wind and waves and cast out demons; surely He could control some fish.

Jesus needed to teach His disciples an important lesson. And in order to learn it well, they first had to experience "failure."

Imagine yourself on the shore that morning when Jesus says:

"Friends, haven't you any fish?"

"No," they answered.

He said, "Throw your net on the right side of the boat and you will find some." (John 21:5–6)

Scripture doesn't record the disciples' thoughts, but I imagine they were frustrated and a bit annoyed at this piece of advice. After all, they'd been doing everything they knew to do. Why should they keep trying? The fish obviously weren't there!

Have you ever felt that way about your life? You've done everything you know to do, but nothing changes?

The disciples were about to learn an important lesson about the source of power to make changes! Even though they didn't recognize Jesus physically, I'm confident they heard His voice in their hearts. They obeyed Jesus's directive, and Scripture records, "When they did, they were unable to haul the net in because of the large number of fish" (John 21:6).

Scripture tells us at that moment they recognized the Lord, and the disciples brought in the boat, towing the fish behind. I love that God had this detail recorded about the catch: "It was full of large fish, 153, but even with so many the net was not torn" (v. 11).

The disciples didn't just have success, they had great success.

This would have been a non-story had the disciples ignored the suggestion to do things differently. They could have insisted they knew how to fish, they knew the water, and they knew the behavior of the fish. And yet they humbly listened and obeyed.

The blessing of the fish was minor in comparison to seeing Jesus and His power at work in their lives again.

There are so many rich lessons in this passage, but what I want us to focus on is that Jesus needed the disciples to see the difference between self-directed effort and Jesus-directed effort. And in order to show them, He let them fail on their own first.

Oh, how I need to learn this lesson myself. I wonder if Jesus has watched me try on my own and held back success while I do. Is He just waiting for me to listen for His voice? To take my direction from Him first?

For us "can do" people, this is a lesson to let soak deep in our spirits. Yes, we *can* do many things on our own, but that doesn't mean we should. Why would we choose to ignore the greatest source of wisdom and power ever known in exchange for our comparatively paltry efforts?

When we operate in our power, we will see only what we can do. When we operate under the direction of Jesus and with the power of the Holy Spirit, we will see what God can do.

This lesson has profoundly impacted my life. Rather than doing what I've always done based on my own ideas and experience, my life is radically different when I ask Jesus for His direction. Not just once but daily.

If you are new in asking the Lord for direction, it can be hard to know if He's answering or if it's you. Here's how I've learned to hear the Lord's voice. First, I choose to believe He will answer. His Word says He promises wisdom, and that's what I need (James 1:5). Believing that is true, I ask my question and wait for an answer.

Sometimes I hear nothing. So I'll wait, listening for His answer. Sometimes I have several thoughts and I don't know which is right. So I'll watch and wait again for confirmation.

Sometimes I have a thought so clear and focused I'm sure it's His answer. If it doesn't contradict Scripture or the character of God, then I accept it is God speaking to me through His Spirit and I make that choice.

As I look back on my life, the times I've seen God work in the greatest ways are when I've restrained my instincts to plow ahead and stopped to ask for His help. It's only when I admit my natural strength isn't enough that His supernatural strength is evident.

This is such a simple principle but so hard to implement for busy women. When left to my own instincts, I launch myself into work first thing without pausing to check in with my Source of help.

Isn't it amazing that the best productivity tip doesn't involve working, but rather pausing, listening, asking, waiting? As the disciples learned that morning on the lake, we are never far from success when we allow Jesus to direct our choices.

Identify God's Priorities for My Life

As I shared earlier, it wasn't until I got to Charlotte and connected with Proverbs 31 Ministries that I ever thought of "ministry" as what happened in my home. I thought it was all about what I did for others. I also never thought about the person I was becoming.

This attitude created an external focus on priorities that drove me to do more. And there will always be more to do.

I wanted to serve God, and I truly thought I was. But my crumbling heart and erratic schedule revealed misplaced priorities.

My core values weren't identified, and when you build a life from the outside in, you will fall apart. I had to learn to rebuild myself from the inside out. And part of that meant identifying God's priorities for me, but this wasn't easy.

With so many good opportunities in my life, it felt almost impossible to identify what was God's best. Every day we are faced with unlimited needs from friends who are hurting, children who need support, and a world that's desperate for hope and help. Can we possibly know God's will for us?

I believe it's possible. In fact, Scripture confirms this. Romans 12:2 says, "Do not conform to the pattern of this world, but be transformed by the renewing of your mind. Then you will be able to test and approve what God's will is—his good, pleasing and perfect will."

When you build a life from the outside in, you will fall apart.

Our minds are renewed by spending time alone with God and spending time in His Word. When we fill our minds with the things of the world, we will conform to that pattern. And the pattern of the world creates a search for external significance and worth that can lead to being overbusy.

But God's ways are different. His will for us always involves peace because He is the God of peace.

To try and establish a healthy pattern of identifying my priorities, I came up with five questions. These questions help me establish my core list of responsibilities and serve as a filter when other opportunities arise.

1. What can only I do?

There are some jobs in my life no one else can do. For example, no one else can nurture my personal faith in God. I'm the only one who can sit myself down every day and spend time with the Lord. I'm the only one who can pray and read the Bible.

No one else can build my inner character. The choices I make with my thoughts, the biblical values I embrace—only I'm responsible for these. Will I be honest? Will I choose grace over judgment? A friend can't do this for me.

I'm also the only wife my husband has. Unless I'm willing to abdicate that role, being a godly wife is a high priority. God has also given me five children to mother, and that is a high calling and an honor. Plus, no one else can take care of my health. It's my responsibility to eat the right foods and stay as healthy as I can. Those five areas of life (plus a few others) are no-brainers to me and will always be at the top of my priority list.

2. What has God entrusted to me?

This question is somewhat similar to the first, but it involves identifying what God has given me to manage. We've all been entrusted with something. First, we have our natural gifts, such as intelligence, physical talents, inherent abilities, and spiritual gifts. Then we have homes, jobs, and existing volunteer commitments. These are givens we need to prioritize.

I want to clarify that as we discuss being overbusy, the job and volunteer commitments might change as we edit our lives to be balanced. But for most of us, these are part of God's trust.

3. Am I a good steward of what I already have?

This is where I do a painful assessment of reality from questions one and two. How am I doing with what God has already given me? Is my faith weak, my character a mess, my finances a wreck? Have I neglected my husband? Have I honored my parents?

God is always watching to see how I'm doing with what He's already given me. When He sees I manage things well,

He entrusts me with more. When I'm neglectful, the opposite happens.

4. What passion (or dream) has God put in my heart?

The first three questions are the base of my priorities. For me, these must be addressed in order before taking on other responsibilities. But for most of us, God doesn't stop at that. There is kingdom work to be done, and God chose us to carry it out.

Because He is a kind Father, God gives us assignments that we were created to do. And often this involves putting a dream in our heart. This dream can be anything. Some women dream of raising kids, others dream of having a career, and some have a ministry placed on their heart.

I have a young twenty-something friend who has a dream for the country of Rwanda. Emily isn't from there and didn't know anyone who was. Yet somehow God planted the people of Rwanda in her heart. A few years ago she decided to sponsor a young Rwandan girl through Compassion International. Just this month, Emily headed to Rwanda on a mission trip and got to meet her sponsored child, who is now eighteen. Before leaving, Emily made a comment that stuck. She said she felt like she was going home.

I work every day with women who have a dream to write. Usually it's a vague dream, as they don't know what it's supposed to look like. As they step out in faith and seek training in the practical side of the writing craft, God brings the shape of their dream to life.

Only God can place those kinds of dreams in our hearts. Sadly, many of us can't even identify a dream. Perhaps it's buried in your heart, but it's there, and when you unearth it you will experience that sense of completeness that Emily felt.

5. *What has God asked me to do that I haven't done yet?*

This is where it gets touchy. I clearly remember when my pastor made this statement: "God has asked some of you to do something and you haven't done it yet."

My heart started pounding as I felt like a spotlight had turned on me. I knew God had told me to write a book, and I'd had one reason after another not to do it. That day I knew God was reminding me of something He'd already asked me to do, and I needed to respond.

I once heard this statement: "Old orders are standing orders." Meaning, if God asked you to do something years ago and didn't revise the directions, He still expects you to do it. It's never too late to be obedient.

Take Time to Plan

Planning is one thing most highly productive people do differently. And yet most of us resist planning. It requires mental focus that is in short supply. It may require research, which is overwhelming. And it takes time we believe we don't have.

We'd much rather just get started! But what if pausing, praying, thinking, and then planning would make us more effective? What if we could really make changes by thinking about things first?

Planning is the most underrated tool, but it's one that would save us everything we think it will cost us: time, money, frustration, and more.

Have you ever tried to have a vacation without planning? My spontaneous friends scoff at the amount of planning my family does for vacations. But the one time we tried to "wing it" was the time we were the most frustrated. We hadn't researched entertainment options, operation hours, what things would cost, etc. We wasted so much precious time on vacation trying to figure things out.

Planning allows you to prepare for the worst so you can enjoy the best.

Planning allows you to prepare for the worst so you can enjoy the best.

For those of us committed to doing things differently, we must carve out time to think and plan. And we must cover it all in prayer. I will often include planning in my quiet time with God. I grab my Bible and to-do list and seek His direction.

Here are some examples of how prayerful planning can benefit you:

- You want to eat healthier? Plan a weekly menu.
- You want to save money? Review grocery sales to make your menu.
- You want to save time? Make a shopping list for your weekly menu before going to the store.
- You want more peaceful mornings? Write your morning tasks, assigning a time for each.
- You want to watch less TV? Plan what you will do instead (read your Bible, read a novel, work a jigsaw puzzle, write your grandma a letter).
- You want to get to the gym? Plan your schedule for the week and make an appointment with yourself.

- You want to write more? Again, get your schedule and make an appointment with yourself.
- You want to spend more time with your spouse? Research things you can do together, then get them on the schedule.

Many of us have bigger goals we believe we'll never accomplish. Maybe it's a mission trip, homeschooling, changing careers, going back to school. There is no way those things happen without planning.

If you aren't a planner, start small. Identify one area of your life that consistently feels out of your control and spend some time just thinking about it. Daydream even. Identify where you want to go or what you want to happen. Then, using that as your goal, identify the steps needed to get there. Write them down so you have it as a record.

God made our brains to be creative and solve problems. We just need to give ourselves time to let them work. So find a few moments just to think today.

Keep a Master List and a Daily List

My final tip for peaceful productivity is one that revolutionized my life in a very practical way. It involves keeping a master list of everything I need to do and pulling from that to create my daily list. I alluded to this concept in chapter 4, but I'd like to go into more depth here.

I mentioned my bookshelf full of time-management books, and one of my favorites is *Getting Things Done* by David Allen. The book is worth reading in its entirety, but I want to share a concept that has helped me the most. Allen identifies a problem most of us encounter when we keep all we have to do on one list. It's simply too much and too complicated, mostly because we put projects and tasks side by side. A project is anything that requires more than one action. A task involves just one action.

For example, I might put "plan Robbie's birthday party" next to "call Liz." Calling Liz is a one-step task. Planning a party involves multiple steps. We sabotage ourselves when we put these things on one list.

After reading the book, and at the height of being over-busy, I did a brain dump. I listed everything I had to do at the moment and in the future. At that time, I didn't worry about separating projects and tasks—I just got it out of my brain.

Creating this list took days and multiple pieces of paper as I remembered one thing after another. When I saw how long the list was, I sat down and had a good cry.

Then I pulled myself together and created a project management notebook. Because I'm old-school, I actually got a three-ring binder. Then I sorted through that brain dump list and separated projects, putting them on separate pages as necessary. The tasks fit on their own page.

Finally everything was in one place. And although it was overwhelming, I felt more at peace than I had in years.

From that master list, I made a very short daily to-do list containing less than I thought I could do each day. This practice actually goes against what Allen teaches, but it's helped me set priorities for each day.

Doing a major brain dump and organizing my work by projects and tasks not only helped me manage my workload, but it was the first time I'd ever listed all my responsibilities in one place. I finally had hard evidence of my addiction to overwork.

After that, I was able to edit my responsibilities. I realized I'd held on to responsibilities that I didn't feel called to do anymore. I had procrastinated on other things that hung over my head for years. It took me a year of finishing projects and resigning from a few volunteer positions, but I was finally able to get my workload under control.

We will never drift into managing our lives well.

Now, about seven years later, I don't need a project management notebook. I still keep a master list of projects and tasks, but it's much shorter. And the three-ring binder sits on my shelf as a reminder of those overbusy years.

We will never drift into managing our lives well. And while there are plenty of productivity tips around, I hope the four I've shared in this chapter will help you as much as they have helped me.

Thirteen

Finding True Soul Rest

As we end our time together, I want to focus on true rest. The kind that settles deep in your soul and brings unexplainable peace. The kind of rest the world doesn't know and isn't connected with circumstances.

Rest can feel elusive. That which should make us feel rested often doesn't. Consider waking up after a restless night and your first thought being how soon you can go back to bed.

Propping your feet on the coffee table after a long day of work and turning on a recorded episode of *Fixer Upper* could make you feel rested. But all it does is make you wish you had an urban country industrial farmhouse. Dissatisfaction taps on your heart and the restlessness begins again.

Vacations really should be a time of rest. But after working overtime to get ready, then the rush of the trip, then working overtime to make up for being gone, restful is not how you would define your vacation.

I've struggled with the biblical definition of rest for years. I hope this book has helped shed some light on God's gift of rest. But if the only definition of rest we remember is the absence of work, then we have missed the fullness of God's gift.

As we end our time together, I want to come back to the words of Jesus. There's something more in His promise of rest that merits a closer look.

Jesus spoke these words that whisper hope to every one of us worn down by the demands of life . . .

> Come to me, all you who are weary and burdened, and I will give you rest. Take my yoke upon you and learn from me, for I am gentle and humble in heart, and you will find rest for your souls. For my yoke is easy and my burden is light. (Matt. 11:28–30)

Jesus invites us to come to Him as the Source of what feels elusive: soul rest.

What Is the Soul?

No anatomy student could tell you where to find the soul. That's because our soul is more than our brain, which controls in minute detail all the activity in our body, including our emotions, reactions, and reasoning. When Scripture speaks of our "heart," as we've discussed in an earlier chapter, this is the core of who we are in our personality and mind. But our soul composes more . . . it's our entire being.

The *Holman Illustrated Bible* explains it this way: "In the Hebrew Old Testament the word generally translated 'soul' is *nephesh*. The word occurs over 750 times, and it means primarily 'life' or 'possessing life.'"[11]

When we see "soul" defined as our lives, then the soul rest Jesus offers has to be all-inclusive. It's more than the promise of a good night's sleep. It's more than the offer of a rest for our mind, which would relieve us from worry or stress. It's not just rest for our spirit, which longs for a connection with God.

Jesus seems to speak to the weariness and burdens that combine these three things. I'm not sure exactly how the body, mind, and spirit connect. But the promise here is of a rest that is all-consuming. A rest that we feel in our minds, in our bodies, and in our spirits. And the only place we will find this rest is Jesus.

Soul rest is deeper than any other kind of rest I've experienced. It's not circumstantial, nor does it need to be renewed. Rather, soul rest has its roots in something unshakable. It is rooted in faith and confidence that we are deeply and unconditionally loved . . . that we are held safe in the arms of our heavenly Father. And nothing, "neither angels nor demons, neither the present nor the future, nor any powers, neither height nor depth, nor anything else in all creation, will be able to separate us from the love of God that is in Christ Jesus our Lord" (Rom. 8:38–39).

Soul rest comes when we trust God fully, which is quite different from *saying* we trust God. Words will not give us the rest our souls long for. Trust will.

Jesus modeled this kind of rest in the middle of chaos. Matthew 8 tells of a boat trip that got rocky: "Then he got into the boat and his disciples followed him. Suddenly a furious storm came up on the lake, so that the waves swept over the boat. But Jesus was sleeping" (vv. 23–24).

Imagine that! Rain is pelting the disciples, water is literally washing over the sides of the boat, filling the bottom, and Jesus sleeps.

The disciples react the same way I would at that point: they panic. "The disciples went and woke him, saying, 'Lord, save us! We're going to drown!'" (v. 25). Fear drives them to wake Jesus, and I imagine it took shaking His shoulder to rouse Him from that deep slumber.

Some kudos go to the disciples, since they obviously knew Jesus could save them. They had some measure of faith at that point in their journey with Jesus. But rather than an "attaboy," they received correction: "He replied, 'You of little faith, why are you so afraid?' Then he got up and rebuked the winds and the waves, and it was completely calm" (v. 26).

"The men were amazed and asked, 'What kind of man is this? Even the winds and the waves obey him!'" (v. 27). By this point in their walk with Jesus, Matthew records that the disciples had seen Him heal every kind of disease and sickness, including the demon-possessed, those with seizures, the lepers, and even those who were paralyzed. They'd heard Him teach with wisdom and authority that no man could obtain. And now He could even command nature?

This was no man. This was God in the flesh, come to seek and find the lost, those whose hearts were far from God, and stand in the place of judgment for our sins so we could have a relationship with God.

This Jesus was Lord of all *then* and is Lord of all *now*.
When we declare Jesus to be the Lord of our lives—meaning He's not just someone we read about in the Bible—something changes in us. And when we learn, believe, and live like He is worthy of our complete faith and trust, then we start to experience the soul rest He offers.

I haven't always felt this rest. More often I have felt the restlessness that comes from trusting myself more than Jesus.

My journey to trust Jesus has taken my entire life. I've always loved Him and I believe He is who He claims to be. But trust? I don't give my trust easily.

People have betrayed me. They've looked me in the eye and promised something they had no intention of honoring. Some had good intentions but found it easier to choose their own way over keeping a commitment. I'm acutely aware of my own failings as well. So my trust always has a "yes, but" attached to it when I give it to a person.

But each time I deliberately choose to trust God—and I refuse to let those "yes, but" thoughts try to sneak in—fear loosens its grip on me. Anxiety recedes. Stress melts away. Worry doesn't consume me. I am a different person than I was ten years ago because of this soul rest that comes from trusting Jesus.

Trust is such an easy word to speak but a harder word to live. I know that. And I don't want to spout easy Christian advice knowing you've heard it a thousand times. Instead, I want to share from my heart what has helped me find soul rest, and that's identifying my source of security.

Insecurity makes us desperate. Have you ever hiked a mountain, only to slip on a steep slope? In that moment of falling, you panic and grab for anything that seems secure.

Security replaces panic with peace. An item is secure when it is attached to something immovable. For example, if I'm camping and secure the tent to the metal tent poles, and the tent poles are secure in the immovable ground, the tent won't fly away at the first gust of wind.

What a difference it makes when we secure the truth about ourselves to the immovable truth of God.

But when something *isn't* secured to an immovable object, there's always the chance of damage when it faces opposition. If I pound tent stakes into sand and a storm arises, sleep will not be possible. Instead, I'll spend my time worrying about the tent flying away, or I'll be up moving it to solid ground.

Insecurity in our lives can be much like this. Our souls long for security, to be grounded in that which will not move. When we aren't grounded, we subconsciously know our foundation is insecure and changing, which causes us to worry and work harder in a vicious cycle. Rest will seem impossible in this state.

But what a difference it makes when we secure the truth about ourselves to the immovable truth of God. That truth can't be shaken by circumstances, because God can't be shaken.

In the midst of war, betrayal, and fear, King David knew the only source of his security was God: "Lord, you alone are my portion and my cup; you make my lot secure" (Ps. 16:5).

We find another attribution of security in Psalm 112:6–8: "Surely the righteous will never be shaken; they will be remembered forever. They will have no fear of bad news; their hearts are steadfast, trusting in the LORD. Their hearts are secure, they will have no fear."

I've identified three areas of security in my life that have helped me find true soul rest: my safety, my future, and my identity.

We Rest When We Fully Trust We Are Safe in the Hands of God

For years fear ruled my life. I've always been cautious and the one to see the danger in any situation. But fear blossomed when I had children.

I remember it clearly. Joshua was just weeks old, and I sat in our pink recliner holding him in a rare moment of sleep—him not me. Josh cried for the first two weeks of his sweet life, until I figured out I had to eat for him to get enough milk.

What had seemed safe pre-baby now seemed like a threat. Two gentle but big dogs. A pool, even with a fence. Light sockets, standing lamps, a fireplace—it all seemed overwhelming as I desperately tried to stop the sobs that caught in my chest. From that moment on, hypervigilance was my watchword, and I never rested.

Fear is like a disease. If unchecked, it will spread. And so it did. Whether it was my own health and safety or my children's, fear consumed me.

As I learned to reassign trust away from untrustworthy things, I experienced soul rest for the first time. Psalm 91 was instrumental in God redirecting my trust to Him. And it's interesting that in the first verse, rest is mentioned:

Whoever dwells in the shelter of the Most High will rest in the shadow of the Almighty. I will say of the LORD, "He is my refuge and my fortress, my God, in whom I trust." (Ps. 91:1–2)

This psalm goes on to speak of how God will protect us when we declare that He alone is our safe place. It also says He will command His angels concerning us.

Before God freed me from the fear of flying, I was on a flight that experienced some turbulence. I started praying and heard in my spirit, "She needs us." I imagined God sitting on a throne and commanding an angel to settle the plane, and peace flooded my heart.

The hard part of praying for safety is the reality of life in this world. Bad things happen every day. Innocent people are hurt and killed. And yet we have the power of God to protect us.

I can't pretend to understand the full impact of sin and free will. But I do know God asks us to come to Him in prayer and seek His protection. And our faith is important. For too long I prayed while not really believing God would answer. This is not faith that pleases God. Faith that pleases Him is that of a child who fully trusts their parent. I'm not even close to that kind of faith, but with God's help, I'm moving closer.

Recently I was speaking with a friend about praying for our adult children. She is a woman of faith, and yet I was surprised when she said that she prays but still worries about bad things happening.

It got me thinking about whether worry and faith have a place together. I don't think God wants them to coexist, but in reality they do. I've experienced it as a process: as one grows, the other diminishes. It's up to us which is which.

Imagine it as a battle, and every time we declare our trust in God, we take a bit more ground from the enemy.

This freedom from worry and fear is worth risking our trust in the One who is completely trustworthy. Not only do we experience soul rest, but the side benefit of this kind of faith is also physical rest. Anyone who has ever stared at the ceiling night after night will appreciate this.

We Rest Knowing Our Future Is Secure in the Hands of God

For seven years my husband and I led our senior high youth group. We loved those kids and spent so much time with them. Retreats, camping trips, pool parties, and lots of time talking about God, the Bible, and life.

One Sunday night, as we sat in a circle talking about the future, Lara suddenly broke down in tears. It took a while until she composed herself enough to share, and even then she was embarrassed. Finally she whispered, "How will I know which pans to use when I'm cooking?"

Thankfully, no one laughed, as we sensed the worry about her future was real. Maybe we also realized each of us had similar worries but weren't brave enough to voice them.

Most of us have worried about the future at one time or another. Will we get married, have children, find the right job, get that contract, lose our job, get sick, etc.? The future is a big unknown, with endless possibilities—good and bad.

While I'm all for wise planning, even the best planners in the world can't predict the future. Only One knows our future and has a plan for us.

In Jeremiah 29:11 we have one of the most popular verses in the Bible regarding the future: "'For I know the plans I have for you,' declares the LORD, 'plans to prosper you and not to harm you, plans to give you hope and a future.'" This verse was spoken by God through the prophet Jeremiah to the people of Israel when they had been exiled to Babylon. This was not God's Promised Land for them, but God reminded them He had not forgotten them, nor had He given up on them.

What a beautiful picture of God's heart for us. No matter how desperate our situation is, how far we've turned from His plan, or how shaky our faith is, God still has a good plan for us.

God continued His reassurance to His people with this promise for their future: "Then you will call on me and come and pray to me, and I will listen to you. You will seek me and find me when you seek me with all your heart. I will be found by you" (Jer. 29:12–14).

When bad things happen, and they might, this does not mean God made a mistake with our future. He's never wringing His hands in worry and thinking, "Oh no, now what will I do?"

God has an eternal perspective on everything. He knows our time on this earth is but a blink compared to the eternity we will spend with Him.

I imagine it's much like a parent who sends their child on a mission trip. We want them to get to know God in a new and fresh way, to learn to trust Him, to develop their calling, to learn to serve others, to learn about themselves, and to come home with a new perspective. Sometimes the hardest times are the best teachers.

I wonder if God feels that way about our time here on earth? I'm confident God hates sin, because He said so Himself. So I know He doesn't love everything that happens here. It must break His heart. But He also doesn't allow anything to be wasted in His plan for us.

Romans 8:28 says, "And we know that in all things God works for the good of those who love him, who have been called according to his purpose." Our eternal home is in heaven, and that is our secure future. And here on earth, no matter what we face, God is working things out for our good when we love Him. Knowing this, we can have true soul rest.

We Rest Knowing Our Identity Is Secure in Christ

In chapter 3 I shared a truth that changed my life: I'm not what I do. For years I had the wrong idea that my worth was connected to my work. So when I did something well, I felt good about myself. When something flopped, so did my self-worth.

But finally, after years of being a Christian, I learned that my worth comes from my position as a dearly loved child of God. My value is not connected to how well I did on a test, or how many women showed up at a Mother's Day Tea, or my title at work.

My identity is not tied to how well I perform as a wife or mother. Nor is my identity connected to how well my children behave, their grades at school or position on the football team, or how successful my husband is.

My worth isn't found in the type of car I drive, my home, or my clothing size. I'm not an employee, leader, volunteer, singer, writer, or teacher. At least not at my core.

One day all these things will pass away.

If I find my identity in any of these fleeting things, I will always be obsessed with doing more. Because there will always be more to do . . . a higher grade, title, or ranking to obtain, more likes on my Instagram posts, a flashier car, trendier clothes, more friends, more experiences. This is exhausting. This is a burden.

We'll never find significance in worldly things, because we weren't created for this world.

There's always some way I can be a better wife, mother, or home manager. If success is my identity measure, then I will relentlessly pursue more success.

My heart hungers for significance. I long to know I have worth, that I'm not a mistake or a waste of time.

We'll never find significance in worldly things, because we weren't created for this world. We were created to be loved by God and to live with Him forever.

We were created to experience the unconditional love of God and to be known fully as His beloved children. Until we experience that love, we will forever be seeking significance outside of our relationship with God.

This is the message that will free each of us to experience the abundant life Jesus offered. Not abundant with work, but overflowing with love and filled with the true soul rest we long for.

Soul rest replaces striving when our identity is secure.

Thank you for joining me on this journey to discover how to do busy better. It is my prayer that as we've walked this path together, you've come to know yourself a bit better. But more important than that, I pray you've gotten to know God better through the saving grace of Jesus, through the care of the Father, and in the power of the Holy Spirit.

Soul rest replaces striving when our identity is secure.

May you experience God's gifts of work and rest as you come into a greater relationship with the Giver of those gifts.

Acknowledgments

To Jesus, my Lord and Savior: thank You for loving me unconditionally. I will love You, trust You, and serve You all my life.

To my family, who I love more than life: thank you for loving me during my crazy years and supporting me as I've wrestled with finding the balance between work, rest, and having fun with you! There's no one I'd rather do life with.

To my mother and sisters: life hasn't always been easy, and we've faced many heartaches, but thank you for modeling a strong foundation in Jesus that is unshakable.

To my team at Proverbs 31 Ministries: thank you, Lysa TerKeurst, for leading Proverbs 31 Ministries well and for praying that God would bring me to Charlotte . . . even though you didn't know my name. You have changed my life.

To my executive team friends: Lisa, Meredith, Danya, Amy, and Barb S.: thank you for inspiring me to become a more godly woman and supporting me in my calling.

To my Word team at Proverbs 31: Barb G., Janette, Tracie, Kenisha, Karen, Suzie, and Steph . . . I love our team! Thank you for being my cheerleaders and encouraging me to write.

To Esther Fedorkevich and her amazing team at Fedd Agency: thank you for believing in me.

To Andrea Doering and the excellent team at Revell: thank you for believing in my message and for partnering with me to share it with others.

Notes

1. Carol Brazo, *No Ordinary Home: The Uncommon Art of Christ-Centered Homemaking* (Sisters, OR: Multnomah, 1995), 24–25.

2. Dictionary.com, s.v. "busy," accessed December 20, 2016, http://www.dictionary.com/browse/busy.

3. Barbara J. Bruce, "Sabbath," in *Holman Illustrated Bible Dictionary*, ed. Chad Brand et al. (Nashville: Broadman & Holman, 2003), 1426.

4. J. Christian Gillan, "How Long Can Humans Stay Awake?" *Scientific American*, June 11, 2016, www.scientificamerican.com/article/how-long-can-humans-stay/.

5. Alan D. Lieberson, "How Long Can a Person Survive without Food?" *Scientific American*, June 11, 2016, http://www.scientificamerican.com/article/how-long-can-a-person-sur/.

6. Kristine Brown, "When Good Intentions Get in the Way," *Encouragement for Today*, January 17, 2017, http://proverbs31.org/devotions/devotion-author/kristine-brown/.

7. John Ortberg, *The Life You've Always Wanted* (Grand Rapids: Zondervan, 1997), 82.

8. Kathleen M. Zelman, "Slow Down, You Eat Too Fast," WebMD, accessed January 3, 2016, http://www.webmd.com/diet/obesity/slow-down-you-eat-too-fast.

9. Marcus Buckingham and Curt Coffman, *First, Break All the Rules* (New York: Simon & Schuster, 1999), 145.

10. Susanne Scheppmann, "Wired Tired," *Encouragement for Today*, August 9, 2004, http://www.oneplace.com/devotionals/encouragement-for-today-devotionals-for-women/encouragement-08-09-04-1277001.html.

11. Chad Brand with Fred Smith, "Soul," *Holman Illustrated Bible Dictionary*, ed. Charles Draper et al. (Nashville: Broadman & Holman, 2003), 1522.

Glynnis Whitwer is on staff with Proverbs 31 Ministries as Executive Director of Communications. She currently oversees and writes for the Proverbs 31 devotions, *Encouragement for Today*, with over 950,000 daily readers, and manages the content for the She Speaks Conference for writers and speakers and COMPEL Training for writers.

She's the author or coauthor of nine other books, including *Taming the To-Do List: How to Choose Your Best Work Every Day*, *I Used to Be So Organized*, *When Your Child Hurts*, and *work@home: A Practical Guide for Women Who Want to Work from Home*. Glynnis has a degree in journalism and public relations from Arizona State University. She and her husband, Tod, live in Glendale. They have five young adult children, ranging from nineteen to twenty-five. She blogs regularly at www.GlynnisWhitwer.com.

glynnis whitwer

Room to Breathe

· · ·

GlynnisWhitwer.com

Proverbs 31
MINISTRIES

If you were inspired by *Doing Busy Better* and desire to deepen your own personal relationship with Jesus Christ, I encourage you to connect with Proverbs 31 Ministries.

Proverbs 31 Ministries exists to be a trusted friend who will take you by the hand and walk by your side, leading you one step closer to the heart of God through:

- Free online daily devotions
- First 5 Bible study app
- Daily radio program
- Books and resources
- Online Bible studies
- COMPEL writer's training:
  WWW.COMPELTRAINING.COM

To learn more about Proverbs 31 Ministries
call **877-731-4663** or visit **www.Proverbs31.org**.

Proverbs 31 Ministries
630 Team Rd., Suite 100
Matthews, NC 28105
www.Proverbs31.org

"With celebrations by seasons and the season's special holidays, family events, and spiritual milestones, among others, *Everyday Confetti* encourages the reader to live life to the fullest, to enjoy and celebrate every moment, every occasion, no matter how small."

—*TheChristianManifesto.com*

Also available from
Glynnis Whitwer

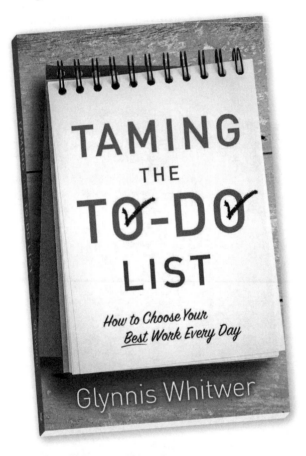

Ever just wish the world would stop for a day so you could catch up? No matter how much we accomplish in a day, we nearly always feel a little guilt over what we didn't do. In *Taming the To-Do List*, Glynnis Whitwer shows you how to be *proactive* rather than *reactive* and take back your schedule by directing your own life!